I0491790

CONTENTS

INTRODUCTION

I will be sharing with you a lot of secrets that I've learned of doing affiliate marketing for over seven years.

Well who am I to indeed instruct you member showcasing, right? Well I have been doing member showcasing for over seven a long time presently, and I have a portfolio of over 11+ websites, separated from that I too do paid counselling, I'm a speaker and a trainer. And presently comes the enormous address, what is member marketing? In member promoting, three parties are involved. There's a vendor or a partner arrange, let's consider it to be Amazon. At that point there will be you, as an affiliate.

Where you will be promoting the products of the merchant through a special affiliate link.

So when someone purchases a product through your affiliate link, you get a commission, that is, you make money.

Now in my affiliate marketing playlist, I'll show you step-by-step on how to sign up to the affiliate network, how to generate your links, how to promote these links to thousands of people for free and then make money from your links.

Almost all popular companies use affiliate marketing to drive customers.

Be it Amazon, Flipkart, Ola, Uber, Swiggy, FoodPanda, Zomato- almost all popular companies are doing it.

But the important question is, how affiliate marketing will help you.

Well the biggest benefit is definitely online earning on **autopilot**.

Today my websites are driving free traffic every month from Google and making me affiliate commission.

So now let's talk about who can learn affiliate marketing.

You don't need any special qualifications; you don't need any technical background.

All you need is one laptop, or a computer, and an internet connection.

This is all you need.

The best part about affiliate marketing is that you are making money from the comfort of your home.

There is no age limit, no massive course fee, only your willingness to learn, and your willingness to earn money online.

I'm friends with people who are making **$100,000 per month to $300,000** per month from affiliate marketing.

So now let's talk about what is the best way to learn affiliate marketing.

Well when I started there was no one to guide me.

No one to tell me the best tips, tricks, tools or strategies that actually work.

Well lucky for you, I'll be teaching you and guiding you in every step.

You need a guide, a person who has made the mistakes, so that you don't repeat those mistakes.

So now let's talk about which affiliate network to focus on.

There are thousands of affiliate networks in the market.

I myself use 50+ affiliate networks to make money for my affiliate websites.

 So which one should you choose?

While there are more complicated ones like Click bank and

the Commission Junction, where you need the knowledge of advanced digital marketing in order to make money.

This is because the competition is just way to high.

For beginners, who are just starting out, the one I recommend is Amazon Associate.

It's easy to run and promote and now I'll be showing you why you should be focusing only on Amazon.in.

Amazon is the world's biggest ecommerce website.

Amazon.com is driving more than 2.5B visitors per month.

Amazon India or Amazon.in is driving more than 360M people per month.

The best part is that every experienced affiliate marketer is only targeting Amazon.com in the US market.

But there's usually zero competition in Amazon India.

So making money from an Indian Amazon associate account is a hundred times easier than promoting in Amazon.com on the US market.

Apart from this, there is many other reasons why you should join the Amazon affiliate network.

Once you promote your Amazon affiliate link the cookie period is for 24 hours.

So whatever the customer ends up purchasing in the next 24 hours, you will be getting the commission for that.

The second good point is that you will be getting paid the affiliate commission for the entire cart.

So let's say you refer someone to buy a t-shirt.

But the person ends up buying a jeans, a cap and the t-shirt as well.

You will be getting the affiliate commission for the entire cart value and not just the product that you recommend.

This is the best part about the Amazon affiliate link.

And since Amazon has so much data and optimization, majority of the people end up buying so many other products and not just the product you recommend.

You can see in the image on the screen that majority of the products that I sold are not the products that I was promoting but the other products that people purchased when I referred them and I still got the commission.

The third benefit is the Amazon brand.

Amazon is now one of the biggest ecommerce website in India.

They spend millions in advertising and now everyone knows about Amazon.

So there's a trust from the consumers from Amazon, so the conversion rate of people buying from Amazon is very high.

This also helps in getting more sales and hence, making more affiliate commissions.

I am getting a massive 3.5% conversion rate.

So every hundred people I refer to Amazon, almost 3 – 4 people end up buying the products.

So that's just amazing.

So now let's talk about how can you make money from affiliate marketing.

The easy answer is create a website and scale it.

Don't worry, I won't just tell you this and end the video, in our next lesson of our affiliate marketing playlist, I will tell you how to select a profitable niche.

In lesson three I'll show you a step-by-step in how to create an Amazon affiliate website like a pro.

I will be sharing all my strategies that I've learned in the last 7 years of building and scaling affiliate websites.

So make sure you watch our complete playlist.

I even created a comprehensive ebook on how to scale an Amazon affiliate website from $0 - $1,000 per month and also how to scale it further to $10,000 per month.

If you want this ebook, all you have to do is like the video, subscribe to our channel and comment with "Yes, I want it" in the comment section below.

Once we reach a thousand likes, subscribers and comments, I will make the link of this ebook public on the description section of this video.

There are many benefits of starting and scaling affiliate websites.

Just as I mentioned, the competition in India is very low.

So if you watched our lessons and follow them to the heart, then I can guarantee that within few months, you will be making money.

You don't even have to work on your website when your article ranks on Google search results.

It's free traffic, month on month.

Unlike other platforms that come and go, Google is not going anywhere.

So you don't have to worry that Google will go out of fashion in a few months.

People will keep on searching on Google.

There are many others ways apart from affiliate links that you can make money from your affiliate website.

You get sponsorship opportunities, branches will start emailing you... you'll also be making money from sponsored links, sponsored reviews.

Like I am charging Rupees, Rs 10,000 – Rs 20,000 for one sponsored review.

And also in the end, let's say you decide you don't like the Amazon affiliate website, and you want to sell it.

Then the website sells for 30x its monthly revenue.

So let's say you're making Rs 10,000 from your website on a monthly basis you can sell it for Rs 300,000.

Now I know that many of you will ask me in the comment section the other ways of doing affiliate marketing.

Like opening a YouTube channel or doing it through Instagram.

So let's take each option one-by-one and share its pros and cons.

So let's start with opening a YouTube channel.

Yes, you can open a YouTube channel in any niche.

Like many other YouTubers are doing, and they are also making good affiliate revenue.

You can create a fashion-related channel and promote fashion-related products.

You can also create a technology-based YouTube channel and promote just like Technical Guruji is doing, but the main point to stress is that YouTube is getting competitive.

Already for all the popular categories, be it fashion, be it gardening, be it technology, already YouTubers are dominating that niche.

It was easier a couple of years back when the competition was low, and also because of the Reliance Jio wave.

Now already majority of the profitable niche has a channel dominating.

Now, I'm not saying that you won't be able to do it.

Yes, you can open a YouTube channel and you will be able to scale it.

But it is extremely difficult.

It will be difficult to scale, you'll have to be patient.

You also have to show your face and you'll also have to invest in expensive equipment.

I will be creating a YouTube marketing course very soon on this channel so make sure you subscribe to get notified about that...

But then again YouTube is more competitive compared to the Amazon alternative that I'm telling you.

Now, let's talk about promoting affiliate links through Instagram.

One thing that I should mention is that every social media platform comes and goes.

So Instagram might not be able to survive in a couple of years.

Also getting followers in 2019 is extremely difficult compared to a couple of years back.

Every social media platforms is going with the pay-to-play mode.

Like the case of Facebook, earlier the organic reach was very high.

So let's say you have 10,000 page likes, if you post a new post, you'll be able to reach that 10,000 people.

But now Facebook wants you to pay money in order to reach the people who even like your page.

Now the competition on Instagram is also growing because the people know that there's money to be made.

And also Instagram wants you to pay money to get those followers.

So the organic growth is down.

And the worst part about Instagram is that there is only one place where you can add the affiliate link that is the bio.

So the number of links of the affiliate links will be far less and hence the oral commission that you make in a month will be much lower.

And this is why I don't recommend Instagram as the only source of promoting your affiliate links.

The same goes for a Facebook page or a group.

The organic reach is dead, so you won't be able to promote your affiliate links in a profitable manner.

So I don't recommend either going into Instagram or YouTube or a Facebook page or a group... rather the smart strategy is to go into a low competition area and dominate it before it gets too competitive.

Also, once your affiliate sites start getting traffic, you can move to these verticals either YouTube channel or Instagram account.

Trust me I've been doing this for almost 7 years, I have tried and tested everything.

The best strategy is to first start a website, scale it, and then move to the various verticals of YouTube and Instagram.

This has given me the best results.

So what is the process of making money from affiliate marketing through a website.

Everything is explained in detail in our affiliate marketing course playlist.

But right now, I'll be giving you a general overview of how all these works.

The process will be something like this.

The first step is to do niche research.

I will help you find a low competition and profitable money-making niche.

Then in the next lesson I'll share with you how to start a pro affiliate website.

I'll be sharing with you my tips, tricks and strategies that I've learned in the last 7 years of doing affiliate marketing.

Also, I'll be telling you the mandatory things that you need to follow so that your account doesn't get banned.

The third step is keyword research.

I'll share with you the exact strategy that I use to find low competition keywords that make you money not in years, but in months.

The fourth step is to write articles.

Either you can write it yourself, but I'll also tell you how you can outsource it to someone else.

I have spent thousands of dollars in knowing the best article structure.

How many words your article should have?

What should be the button color?

I have tested everything.

And I'll be sharing the perfect article template with you in one of the lessons.

The next step will be signing up to the Amazon Associate account.

How to sign up?

How to get approved?

And how to not get banned.

The next lesson will cover the most important detail.

How to get your article on rank number one on Google search results.

So let's say your website is about guitar and you write an article like "best guitars in India".

So I'll share with you all the strategies that I use to rank number one for my target keyword.

And the last step is for you to send me a thank you email for introducing you to affiliate marketing.

I would love to see some success stories if I like your site, I might even collaborate with you for other projects.

So now let's talk about money.

How much many can you make?

Now this depends entirely on you.

How much time you are willing to invest on your website.

The more time you invest, the more money you will be making.

If you follow our complete playlist then I can tell you for sure that you will be making money in few months.

In the beginning, it might look a bit complicated because you are new at this.

But given a few days of implementing, you will become a pro.

Once you scale the website, then you already know all the secrets.

Then you can create many more websites, build a team, and scale even further.

Like I started as a one-man-army, but today I have 9 full time people working on my affiliate websites.

You are planting a tree.

Once it's grown up, all you have to do is spend a few hours on your website and it will keep giving you fruits for many years to come.

Now let's talk about common affiliate marketing mistakes.

New affiliate marketers make these following common mistakes.

Even I made them when I got started.

The first mistake is not showing patience.

You won't start making money on day one.

Rather, slowly and steadily you will be scaling.

The second mistake is not implementing.

Majority of you will just be watching the lessons, but very few of you will be actually implementing.

But the people who implement, will be getting the best results.

So make sure you don't just watch the lessons, but also implement everything I tell you.

And not just implementing, you'll be getting a lot of questions in your mind.

So don't just implement, you can ask your questions in the Facebook group or you can also ask them in our YouTube live sessions.

And I'll try my best to answer all of you guys.

Third mistake is getting greedy.

Now few of you might watch our complete free affiliate marketing course playlist and then start implementing everything on multiple websites.

If you're a beginner or just starting out, even if you are an experienced affiliate, I would recommend you to open only one single website, and try to focus entirely on that.

Your goal should first be able to create a website and scale it.

Learn all the advance strategies, then build a team, and then open multiple websites.

You don't have to work hard, you have to work smartly.

I have already made the mistakes, so you don't have to make the same mistakes again.

Rather follow the working strategies that actually work.

One big advice that I can give to all of you is that practical is what matters the most.

Don't just watch the videos but also implement everything that I tell you in this free affiliate marketing mastery course.

This is the right thing for you guys.

Don't be confused, I am here for you.

I'm so happy to have a new member who will be our future success story.

I'll make sure that this journey of helping you, making money from affiliate marketing is fun, exciting and as easy as possible.

So what are your next steps?

The next lesson of our free affiliate marketing mastery course.

Where I show you on how to scale an Amazon affiliate website from $0 - $1,000 per month.

FREE KEYWORD RESEARCH FOR SEO

So if you would like to understand my keyword research process using free tools, on how I find low competition keywords on for my website then watch this video until the end.

This video is lesson four of our affiliate marketing mastery course where I show you on how to scale an Amazon affiliate website from $0 - $1,000 per month.

Click on the "I" button here to watch all the videos of this playlist.

You should also follow me on Instagram, my username is "DMANKUR" I take live sessions almost every alternative day, where I answer all your questions, so make sure you follow me.

Before doing keyword research you must first select the niche of your website.

If you're watching our affiliate marketing mastery playlist, then you must have already seen our lesson two on niche research.

In this lesson I'll show you ways to seek out a low competition niche for your website.

So I recommend you guys to click on the "I" button here and watch that video first before watching this video.

Once you have finalized your niche, now it's time to find low competition keywords for your website.

Although I personally use a paid keyword tool called "ahrefs".

But since not all of you will be able to afford the expensive tool, I'll be showing you everything through its free alternative.

Which is equally good, and it's called "ubersuggest".

Also if you don't want to waste your time doing keyword research for your website, and want an excel sheet that I created after comprehensively researching about the best low competition keywords.

I have categorized them into low competition, medium competition and high competition and also talked about the profitability of each keyword.

So if you want that excel sheet, all you have to do is like the video, subscribe to our channel and comment with "yes, I want it".

If we reach 1,000 likes, subscribers and comments on this video, I will share the link for the excel sheet on the description section of this video.

So let's go into my laptop screen where I'll show you how to find the right profitable keywords for your website.

Finding the right keywords for your Amazon website is not that difficult, and I'll be showing you the exact process.

Usually I don't follow the same strategy that other SEO experts follow, that they will try to find keywords and they will check its individual competition.

I don't do that.

I'd rather directly go to my competition who is already ranking one on the most keyword, and then I try to find all the related keywords for which he is ranking.

And strategy has helped me scale my website from 0 – 1.2M visitors per month.

So let me tell you how it's done.

So first let's open Ubersuggest free tool by Neil Patel.

So let's say your affiliate website is about best washing machines.

So what you do is, go on to Google, search for "best washing machine in India", okay.

So this is the hook.

So what you have to do is, go to the first website that is ranking number one on Google search results.

So these are the preview snippets.

This is the 0 position, you don't have to take this.

Rather take the first position that is ranking.

So this is from "Bijili Bachao" Open the website... okay, so the article is "best washing machines in India" Copy the URL, paste it here, English/India, select the country as India if you're targeting the Indian audience.

Let's see, go to the top pages....

Now let's find the article that we were searching for, the article is "best washing machine in India" So best washing machine in India is the 2nd most popular in this website and it is ranking number 1.

So best washing machine in India has the potential of 22,000 of traffic.

So let's say we have this here in niche research, let's say we go for washing machine, okay, so the traffic is 22,000, okay.

And washing machine has the percentage of... I have to check it here, I think it's the percentage of appliance, I'm not sure.

It must be 8%... but the conversion rate is 0.01 as I've told you earlier.

Usually the conversion rate of people who visit your website is- 1% actually end up buying the product.

Average selling price of a washing machine is somewhere close to- let's find it out.

So let's open Amazon... and let's go for washing machine.

Right, so average price is somewhere close to around...

Rs13,000, right?

So we'll add the average price to around Rs13,000.

And the commission is 0.08, right?

So let's see, the commission that you will get.

So this result is the multiplication of all of these.

So you will be making a total of Rs22,880 per month, approximately if you're ranking number one.

For your target keyword which is "best washing machine in India".

So the best part about this strategy is all you have to do is click here on "view all" and this will give you the list of all the various keywords for which this article is ranking and also along the position with it.

So for this particular keyword, which is the most popular keyword in the washing machine segment, which has the volume of 14,800... this article is ranking number 2.

Again, best washing machine, number 3.

So this way, all you have to do is click on "export to CSV" and you'll be able to download the complete list of all the keywords for which this article is ranking, right?

So let's see here.

So you were ready to download, almost 220 keywords, right?

And primarily in my research what I've done is that I try to optimize my website for just the top 20 keywords.

Because that alone is more than enough for the Google to understand what the article is about and the rest of the keywords are automatically ranked.

So let's say I am writing an article about the best washing machine in India, what I'll do is- I'll go and find the first ranking article, I'll put it on Ubersuggest, I'll take the highest 20 keywords and optimize my article around those keywords, and that is more than enough guys.

That is the simple process.

Don't make the keyword process too complicated.

And also, stop using Google Adwords.

I've seen so many YouTubers are recommending the Google keyword planner for the keyword optimization, don't do that.

Rather use this amazing tool of Neil Patel.

And the best part is you already know that this website is ranking number 1.

And you already know that this website is driving such an amazing traffic.

So all you have to do is steal the competitor's keywords.

This is better than finding the keywords yourself, right?

And I've been using the same strategy for my affiliate websites and I've been really successful with this strategy as well.

So let me do for another keyword

well.

Okay.

So let's say you go for some other category.

Let's say... we go for "best mobile phone under 10,000".

Okay.

So what we'll do is, we'll go to the first result, which is the 91Mobiles result.

We'll copy the URL.

We'll go to the URL bar paste it here, English / India because we're targeting the India country, select search...okay, it's loading...

though it seems to be a little slow.

So let's wait a bit.

And you can see that there are multiple options as well you'll see the keyword ideas, you can also see the backlinks- okay.

So it's open.

So we are searching for this particular article, right?

The best mobile phones under Rs 10,000.

You can see that it is running 155 traffic.

So all you have to do is find all the keywords for this particular article, because it is already ranking number 1.

Just click on "view all" and this gives you all the keywords for which it is ranking.

Okay, somehow this result is not too good.

So let's check the Digit article, copy it.

Paste it here…and search.

So this article, best phones under 10,000, it is driving 229,000 visitors per month and let's click on "view all" to find all the keywords for which it is ranking.

Best budget smart phone, best budget phone… So these are all the keywords for which it is ranking.

So this is the strategy and similarly you can check the other articles for which this website is ranking as well, like best pones under Rs15,000, etc.

The best particular strategy for finding the right keywords all you have to do is export the keywords and then optimize your article along these keywords.

And you can do to the keyword ideas and find like, "best mobiles" in English and in India… so let's search.

And this will give you a lot of ideas regarding the best mobiles.

Okay, best mobiles… and also the best part about this particular keyword insider is that it will give you the search difficulty... how difficult it is for you to rank your article on number 1 position on Google.

So 66... it's yellow, it's not really too easy to rank because it's a very complicated term because the traffic volume is really high, the competition is also really high.

Similarly, best mobiles under 10,000.

A very high search volume of 110,000 and therefore the competition may be additionally high because 64 is a really high number, right?

SD means SEO difficulty or search engine difficulty, right?

So this is also a great way to find related keywords.

So honestly guys, there's no other complicated technique that you need to know to find the right keywords.

All you have to do is use this free tool called Ubersuggest.

And either you can put URL of your competitor in the search bar and find all its keywords and export it otherwise you can write the keyword yourself and find the ideas along with the search engine difficulty as well.

Because one thing that you have to keep in mind is that keyword is not the only thing that matters.

But the competition level is also what you have to look for.

If the competition of the keyword is high or low, right?

Like you can see here for this particular article the best mobile phones in India for July 2018, this article is driving 110,000 visitors per month.

So this article must be making a lot of money from Amazon affiliate account, right?

So you can see the keywords for which it is ranking, best mobile, best mobile phones.

And also the SEO difficulty like how difficult it is to rank no 1 for this keyword like for best mobile the SEO difficulty is really high, so anything quite 35 or 40 will be difficult for one man army... if you yourself are doing the SEO, writing the articles and everything.

It will be difficult for you to rank number 1.

Not at least a month... it will take at least a year or more than a year.

But if the ranking- SEO difficulty is less than... somewhere close to 30 – 40 or maybe less than 30, then it will be much easier for you to rank no 1 and make affiliate commission.

This is why the niche research video is why I really want you guys to watch it again, because it's the combination of the niche research- you would want to go into a niche which, where the competition is low.

And if the competition I mean the SEO difficulty is low in order that you'll be ready to rank your articles as number 1.

At the same time, the profitability of the niche should be higher.

That is the percentage commission you'll be getting for every person who buys the product from your link is high.

At least in the range of about 5.

Like 5%, 8% or 10%.

Apart from that you can- usually I don't do this, but still you can do this, like if you're looking for "best washing machine in India", okay.

So here also- you'll get some suggestions... you can also load these keywords as well in your excel sheet.

The final excel sheet of the keywords that you want to optimize.

You can use the suggestion bar as well.

You can also add a space here, before "washing" and this will give you any other word that is before "washing machine in India".

You can also optimize for this.

And also at the bottom of the articles you will find various other keywords.

So this is another technique to find related keywords for your target article.

But the one I would recommend is to use Ubersuggest and download all the keywords, that is export the keywords and that is more than enough.

You don't have to make keyword research too complicated guys and still if you have any questions regarding keyword research all you have to try to to is comment below this video and I'll make sure I'll reply to you within 6 hours to 12 hours.

And I'll solve all your doubts.

I really want you guys to succeed and create a profitable Amazon associate website for yourself and share your success story in our Facebook group or whether email it to me.

Directly share your success story with everyone else so that they can also get inspired.

I really want you guys to succeed.

So this is often the right process to seek out the keywords and you don't have to make it complicated, just follow this and that is more than enough for you guys.

If Ubersuggest is something that you don't like and you want to use something else, then you can also try this Chrome extension called "Keywords Everywhere".

It's a free extension and whenever you are searching for a keyword like this, it will show you related keywords on the right side of your desktop or the laptop screen here.

Like I'll search for... let's say I search for this best washing machine in India, and it showed me all the related keywords.

Along with the search volume and the CPC and the competition as well.

Okay, you can also export these keywords as well from "export CSV" option.

So this is another option that you can use to download the keywords and match the competition and if you want to spend some money and you really want the best SEO metrics out there then I recommend "ahrefs".

I've been using it for many years now, it's the best SEO tool out there.

I know it's really expensive but it has a free trial of $7 per 7 days.

So if you want do it what you- you can follow the same procedure like I mentioned in the Ubersuggest.

So all you have to do is copy the article title (URL) go to site explorer, enter it here... make it select URL and search the article.

And it is showing you that this article is driving approximately 15k traffic and the number of referring domain is 3 so yes, the competition is not that high, the competition is low.

And to find the right keywords for which it is ranking, all you have to do is go to the organic keywords section and this will show you all the keywords for which this article is ranking on which position.

Like the main primary keyword is "best washing machine in India" and that it's ranking number 1.

And the volume is 14,000, and similarly you will find all the related keywords for this article as well.

And you can again export this keyword list by clicking here on "export" and download the list.

So this is another method that I highly recommend also it gives the keyword difficulty.

In Ubersuggest the keyword difficulty is less than closer to 35 is more relatable, but here ahrefs has a different metric.

Here the keyword difficulty less than 10 means that the competition will be extremely low and you can directly write an article about this particular keyword and get it ranked on Google easily.

And also since the commission rate is high for this particular niche and also the search volume is significantly high because 14,000 is a excellent search volume, you'll be able to make good money if you're targeting this particular niche.

And… you can also use ahrefs.

Apart from that you simply also can use the keyword explorer here for ahrefs again.

Select "India" and write "best washing machine" and search for it.

And it'll offer you tons of keyword ideas related to this like here it says that the best washing machine has a keyword difficulty of 16 which is medium.

So it's a good keyword you can target it.

And again the main keyword being "best washing machine in India" with 14,000 volume.

And also the best part about this is like if you click on any of the keywords here, it will tell you all about the search result metrics that are already ranking on Google and the competition level on each of them.

Like we are searching for "best washing machine in India".

If you go here, this is the search result.

Like we have a featured snippet, like- this is the featured snippet, right?

The no :1 article which is ranking is from the google Bijili Bachao.

It has 3 referring domains and 3 backlinks.

Similarly, the 2nd article has 9 referring domains and 14 backlinks.

And all of these… and it also tells you the amount of traffic that each article is getting, right?

So this feature is really helpful for me and this is why I use ahrefs because Ubersuggest gives you a more overview, but then again Ubersuggest is free and you don't have to pay any money.

But if you really want to scale your Amazon affiliate website then I highly recommend you guys to invest some money in ahrefs, because this tool will really make your like easier it will- and the best part is its backlink database is tremendous, so you can easily use it to find backlink opportunity and get your article to the number 1 position.

Because yes, keywords matter a lot but apart from that you also need good quality backlinks.

And also this feature I really like because you directly get a picture of the competition of what kind of backlinks you need.

And also now that we have selected the keywords, so now you must be thinking, okay, Ankur I have the keywords, I have followed your technique, I've used Ubersuggest I've used Keywords Everywhere, I've used ahrefs, now I have the perfect list of keywords, I also know the competition level... now how should I write the article?

I want to know how to write the article, right?

So we have a separate video on how to write the perfect SEO-friendly article it is in the same playlist of the affiliate marketing mastery playlist and in that particular video I'll be showing you exactly how to write the perfect SEO article so you'll rank your article even without backlinks.

Even in that, the primary strategy will be looking at your competition and writing an article better than that.

Now again, since we're talking about keywords, look at the number 1 result, this is the article ranking number 1 for our target keyword.

You can see how well he has optimized his article.

Like you can see that the most keyword "best washing machine in

India" that's how he started the article.

Okay, the most keyword is true , and therefore the title as well.

And also he has bolded, like "best washing machine brands in India" "Top Models"..."best washing machines in India"... he has bolded the keyword, so to put more stress.

And this is how he has optimized his article around the keyword.

I will be talking more about this in our SEO-friendly article video.

So make sure you watch that video as well in this playlist.

And make sure you watch the entire playlist because you'll be getting a lot of value and a lot of knowledge about keyword research, building backlinks, SEO and more than that.

So now let me go through the mistakes that people make while selecting keywords.

So the first mistake that people make is that they select keywords with high competition just because the search volume is really high.

So if you go for a keyword like let's say "best mobiles".

Again the competition is comparatively a little higher.

Like best mobiles in the 15,000- yes the search volume is a little higher but then again look at the backlinks of this particular website has who is ranking number 1.

He has 31 referring domains.

If you're a single person who doesn't have a team, you'll be doing the SEO yourself, creating 31 backlinks will be difficult.

It looks easy, but trust me guys it's difficult especially in 2019 when creating backlinks is very, very hard.

This is why I mentioned this multiple times in the niche selection video of our affiliate marketing playlist.

Where I tell you to go for a niche which has a high commission rate but again the competition is low.

Because if you're single-handedly building the website, targeting a high competition niche will be extremely difficult for you because you don't have a team.

You don't have the resources.

And in the end you'll end up losing money.

So make sure you go for the low competition or a medium competition niche and similarly look for the low competition and medium competition keywords so that you'll be able to scale the website to such a level that you are making good money.

So what are your next steps?

Click here to watch the next lesson.

And click here if you want to watch our complete affiliate marketing mastery course, where I show you ways to scale an internet site from $0 - $1,000 per month.

HOW TO CREATE AMAZON AFFILIATE ACCOUNT

I'm making more than $200/month from my Amazon associate account on **autopilot.**I don't have a You-Tube channel, rather a website where my articles are ranking number 1 on Google search results and generating an income, albeit I don't work for months.

In today's video, I will be telling you about how to become an affiliate to Amazon, how to create an account, how to get approved, how to generate links, the way to not get banned from Amazon associate account, and in the end, I'll be taking common questions related to Amazon associate account.

This video is lesson 6 of our free Amazon affiliate marketing mastery course, where I teach you ways to scale an internet site from $0 - $1,000/month.

If you want to watch all the lessons, click on the "I" button here.

You should also follow me on Instagram, my username is "DMANKUR", I take live sessions almost every alternate day where I answer all your questions, so make sure you follow me.

Make sure you watch this video until the top , because I'll be sharing with you everything related to Amazon associate account.

So without wasting any time, let's go into my laptop screen and get started.

Hey guys, I hope that you've already done your niche research, you have selected the right keywords by watching our keyword research video, you've also purchased a hosting and also claimed your bonus offers of free paid theme and free paid plugin.

And I hope you've got written those 5 – 10 articles by watching our SEO-friendly article video of our affiliate marketing playlist.

Because if you're applying to become an affiliate of Amazon, through Amazon associate, your application will not be approved if you don't have content on your website.

So confirm you watch the remainder of the teachings in our Amazon marketing playlist, implement the same and then watch this video again to apply for the Amazon associate account.

So the first step is to search for the "amazon associate" here.

And click here on the Amazon.in associate, this is the place where you can sign up to become an affiliate of Amazon.in.

So the process of becoming an affiliate is fairly simple.

All you've got to try to to is click here on "join now for free".

So if you have already got an Amazon account you can login to your account and then apply, or you can create a new account by clicking here.

So I'm creating a new account for this.

So all you have to do is fill-in your details here and click on "create your Amazon account".

So to your email address there'll be an OTP sent, just enter the OTP here to verify your account.

After this the process of creating your associate will start.

So the very first thing is to feature your pay name here.

In the pay name you've got to feature an equivalent that is on your bank account.

Because there are 2 modes of withdrawal of money from Amazon Associate account.

The first is cheque and the second is NEFT.

For both the things you need the correct payee name.

So make sure you add it correctly.

After the payee name you have to add the address.

And everything else, the postal code, and then your phone number.

And who's the main contact for this account?

Make sure this one is selected.

And for the US tax purpose, are you a US person, select "no" because we live in India.

So fill all these information and click on next.

So here's the section where you have to add the website on which you will be promoting the Amazon affiliate links.

So if you're following our Amazon affiliate marketing course, then you know that we have created a website called "bestdslr.in".

So, I will be adding that domain, here.

So click on "add".

Click on the "next" Now this section talks about a tracker or an ID that you simply are going to be creating, that will be associated with your account.

So you can add anything here, so I'll just add "bestdslr" here.

It is not mandatory that you get the same ID, because it depends on the availability of this ID.

So here you have to add the information about... what your website is about and all.

So I'll just mention a few things here.

After this you have to select which of the following topics best describe your website or mobile app.

So select one of the topics, which... exactly- select any of the category which comes on your website domain.

So for me it's gonna be technology, and the second topic could be photography.

"What type of Amazon items do you intend to list on your websites or mobile apps?" You can find all of them or a few of them depending on what you are actively promoting.

I'll be selecting all of them.

"What type are your websites or mobile apps?" So select what exactly your website is about.

So it's a content or niche website.

So I'll be selecting that and the secondary type, I'll select more likely a "blog".

So how does one drive traffic to your website?

So this section talks about how you will be driving traffic to your website.

Since we are primarily focusing on SEO and somewhat on social media so we'll be these.

"How do you utilize your websites to generate income?"

So select your primary income source.

So you can select that Amazon associate is the only monetization you'll be using.

And for the secondary, you might be going for the display advertisements.

Here they are talking about backlinks, how you'll be building backlinks for your website.

So here you can select "blog editor" because you'll be using WordPress.

How many total visitors does your websites and apps get per month?

Although your website is new and you only have a few articles on your website and also you do not start doing the SEO, so you might be receiving less than 500.

So you can mention this, "less than 500".

What is your primary reason for joining the Amazon associate program?

So here you can mention, "to monetize my website".

And how did you hear about us?

You can mention anything.

Like a blog post or anything else.

Here you just have to fill the captcha,

Click on you agree to the terms, and click on "finish".

Once you are done, there will be one option of entering your payment and tax information.

You can do it later as well, as of now I'll click on "later".

And this is often the Amazon Associate ID that has been given to me, "bestdslr-21".

So whenever someone purchases through my link and if this idea is present in the link, I will be getting the commission of that purchase.

So I'll click on later.

So this is often how the backend of your Amazon Associate will look.

And Amazon also gives you a fast guide how to select the country, how to access the account settings and everything else.

So I'll just show it to you quickly.

So this is the snapshot of your account.

How you'll be making money, how much money you'll be making.

Total items shipped, total earnings, the total ordered items, total clicks, etc.

There are some quick recommendations of the products that you can promote.

And let's go to the account settings, you can here- click here on "account settings".

Here you will find the settings related to your account, like change your password, change your account, add more websites, edit your website information- everything else.

And now let's go to the report section.

What will be do is take you to my Amazon Associate account for one of my Amazon Affiliate website and show you everything... with real data.

So here you can see one of the Amazon Associate account for one of my affiliate website.

And you'll see for the last month, almost 102 products where shipped.

The total earning was around somewhere close to Rs 8,000.

And yesterday itself you'll see that we sold a product, or rather a few products I'm not sure.

Where the fees on my commission was around Rs 1,000.

To check the detailed report, all you have to do is attend the report section here.

Here you will get the complete report of your Amazon Associate account, like how many products where shipped, what particular date.

You can see that on a daily basis I am driving significant amount of clicks and the order revenue, what's my conversion rate?

How many people where ordering product directly through my link.

Or other products they ordered when they visited the website.

And also the refund rate, you'll see that almost 13 to almost 10% refund rate is in India.

And the conversion rate and the item revenue, and my affiliate commission.

This is not the final commission because of the commission gets logged after a few days.

So there might be a few refunds in the future.

So this is often not the precise commission, but it will be somewhere close to this.

You can also go to the "earnings" section.

Exactly on a per day basis, what proportion I'm earning.

From Amazon Associate, from this website.

And you can also change the date range and everything else.

You can also download the reports and- there's so many options.

So i actually request you guys to see all the options, and get comfortable with this dashboard.

Now I'll show you how to generate links for the products that you are promoting.

The best way is to use the site, right?

So after you login to your Amazon Associate account, open Amazon.in.

And the best part is, they'll have this new bar at the top.

It's called Amazon Associate SiteStripe.

So with this, creating the link becomes extremely easy.

Let's say you can click on any product.

Okay... so let's click on this OnePlus 6.

So all you have to do to create an affiliate link for this product, is to click here on text.

You can get the full link here, you can get the short link here.

If you would like the image to even have the affiliate link you can embed the image as well.

So you'll use this, to urge the image.

Or you can choose text and image both.

I use the text link and I usually shorten it.

To find the commission rate on each product the category that on Amazon.in all you have to do is Search for "Amazon Commission Affiliate" and click on this first link.

And this particular page lists down all the particular niche or categories on Amazon and what is the commission rate for each category.

I also showed you this on the niche research on how to finalize the niche and also on the keyword research section.

So this is often how you generate the links and you can add that links to your Amazon affiliate website, and I already showed you how to write the article, an SEO-friendly article in my other video.

So make sure you watch that video.

And just like I mentioned, that too- don't apply to Amazon Associate Account unless and until you have at least 6 – 10 articles on your website.

Otherwise, your application will be denied.

And also later in the video, I'll be telling you many different ways, why Amazon will ban your account.

Many people are getting their accounts banned because they are not following the terms and conditions.

So confirm you watch the video until the end, if you don't want your account to get banned.

So now I've told you everything related to Amazon Associate Account.

How to create it, how to generate links.

Now, there is one important question that needs to be answered.

How to avoid getting banned from the Amazon Associate Account.

I myself have been banned.

My friends have been banned.

And I want to make sure that your account doesn't get banned.

So make sure you watch the rest of the video as well.

The number 1 point is that you have to make 3 qualifying sales from your Amazon Associate Account within 180 days of signing up.

So if you create your Amazon Associate Account the moment you create your website, then there are higher chances that you won't be able to generate those sales within 180 days.

So my recommendation are going to be for you to make a website, write the content, add your article, and once you start getting traffic to your blog, then you should apply for Amazon Associate Account.

Now let's talk about point 2.

This reason is very common among affiliates for their account to get banned.

You cannot use product images from Amazon.

Neither can you copy them.

Neither can you screenshot them.

Neither can you save them into your download folder then use it on your website.

Many of students who are active Amazon affiliates, they have talked to the Amazon care representatives and they have specifically told them not to use the images.

The number 3 point is you're absolutely prohibited from using any link short or a link cloaking service.

So if I even have an Amazon link, and that i use "Bitly:" to shorten it, it is not okay.

Because Amazon wants to be able to see the page sending the traffic.

And also Amazon wants that whenever the user hovers over a link, they should know exactly where they are going to go.

The fourth point is that you are not allowed to use to your own Amazon affiliate link or to encourage your friends or family to use them.

So if you use your own affiliate link to view an item or your friends do that, then this is the sure short thanks to get your account banned.

The fifth point is that you cannot encourage your website visitors to click on the affiliate link just to support the website.

So even if you're writing a simple sentence, something like "by using our affiliate link you'll support the website".

This will get your account banned.

The sixth point is your website should be publicly available where the Amazon affiliate links are shown.

So if you're promoting your Amazon affiliate links inside a membership portal, where a user needs to login then you cannot do it.

The seventh point is that you cannot post any screenshot of any of the customer review or the star rating, or any other things from the Amazon website on to your website.

Okay guys, I think it's taking too long for all the reasons, so what I'll do is I'll go through all the rest of the reasons quickly.

You cannot present yourself as Amazon.

So you cannot quote anything like "you are representing Amazon" or any customer care executive from Amazon.

You cannot do that.

Now the next one is very important because many people make

the mistake.

You cannot use Amazon affiliate links in the email.

So if you have an email list and you are promoting your Amazon affiliate links in your email, your account will get banned.

So the only solution is to drive the people to your website, then you can show the affiliate links on your website.

Likewise you cannot have affiliate links in PDFs or ebooks.

Also you cannot list prices from Amazon.

So if you're quoting a price then your account will get banned.

So stand back from listing the costs of the product.

You also cannot post your affiliate links in someone else's forum.

So let's say you are part of an online community or a forum, you cannot post your affiliate links there.

Also if you have a website and you are using a pop-up plugin, you cannot post an Amazon affiliate link, on a popup.

Also stay away from generating clicks using a software or a bot.

This will get your account banned.

And lastly, you cannot provide any kind of a reward or an incentive to your audience to click on your links.

So if you're following all these guidelines, your account won't get banned.

Now let's talk about a few other questions people have regarding Amazon Associate Account.

So when will you receive the payment from Amazon?

Amazon will pay you approximately 60 days following the end of each calendar month.

So what's the minimum threshold to urge paid?

It's Rs1,000 for any of the transaction and Rs2,500 for the cheque transactions.

And just like I said, you have 2 modes of payment, either you can add your bank account, or get paid through cheque.

Now let's talk about taxes on Amazon income.

The tax rate is same, as if you are self-employed in any other field.

At the top of the year, Amazon will send you a tax form, which will include the revenue that you made in that year.

This number is what you report when you file your tax.

So what are your next steps?

Click here to observe subsequent lesson, and click here if you would like to observe our complete affiliate marketing mastery course where I teach you how to scale a website from $0 - $1,000/ month.

HOW TO CREATE AMAZON AFFILIATE WEBSITE

I will also show you how to get a paid affiliate theme and a caching plugin which combined costs $100 for free,
This is lesson 3 of our free affiliate marketing mastery course.

Starting an affiliate website, was the best decision of my life.

This is all possible because I took the most important decision of starting a website and later, monetizing it.

It took me many years to learn what works and what doesn't.

But lucky for you, I have shared all my working tips and tricks in this affiliate marketing mastery course on YouTube.

So that you don't have to waste any money or time, so that you can directly apply what is working.

Whenever you are building a site, the first step is to register a domain name.

So what is a domain name?

A domain name is an internet address.

An address where internet users can access your website.

Like the case of Facebook, "facebook.com" is the domain name for the company Facebook.

And similarly, "google.com" is the domain name for the company, Google.

I know it's very simple, but still I am explaining for all the people who don't know it.

There can be multiple extensions of your domain name, but the popular one is ".com".

Like "google.COM... facebook.COM... or instagram.COM".

Now ".com" domain extension is more suited for global audience.

But when you're targeting a specific country, like the case of India.

If you're targeting the Indian audience, then instead of going for the ".com" domain extension, you will go for ".in".

Like in my case, my website address is: "ankuraggarwal.in".

Because I'm targeting the Indian audience.

So instead of going for a ".com" domain extension, I went for the ".in" domain extension.

Similarly, let's say if you're targeting Brazil.

Then your domain extension will be ".br".

So in my case it will be "ankuraggarwal.BR".

Now after a domain name, to start a website, you need a hosting.

So what is a web hosting?

A web hosting is a service, where organizations or individuals can post a website or a webpage on the internet.

So just like you have Almira (Indian storage company) to store all your stuff, your website also needs some space to store all the files and the folders.

A website is nothing but a directory of files and folders that are rendered through a server of a particular domain name.

So whenever you are thinking of starting a blog, you need 2 things, first is the domain name, and second is the website hosting.

So whenever you are buying a website hosting, you're actually buying a space on a server.

So now there are various companies that sell website hosting.

Like SiteGround, BlueHost, GoDaddy and HostGator.

So whenever you are a buying a website hosting, you are actually buying a server space of these companies.

So these companies have massive servers.

So you're actually paying a monthly fee, for access to some space on these servers.

So whenever we are talking about a shared webhosting, you're actually taking some server space of the server.

Because taking the entire server will be really expensive, so shared hosting is the solution for all the people who want to start their site at a very cheap price.

Now let's talk about the free hosting.

Free is always preferred by people.

And they also think why pay for a hosting, when they can get it for free, right?

But you have to understand one thing, there's nothing free in this world.

Yes, free hosting does exist.

But they have their limitations.

Their drawbacks are honestly, not worth it.

Especially when you're starting an affiliate website to make money.

You need an extra edge to beat your competition.

So if you're starting an affiliate website, you need to invest in a paid hosting.

Free hosting providers like Blogger or Wix have certain limitations.

You cannot customize your website like the way you want, there will be a subdomain instead of your primary domain, and the worst of all, there is no technical support.

Since you're starting out a new website, sooner or later you will face issues.

You will face problems like installing WordPress, some plugin is not working, or maybe your website is not rendering.

You need someone to talk to, someone who can help you.

This is where the paid hosting companies come into play.

They have support people.

You can call them, you can live chat with them and they will solve your issues within minutes.

But with free hosting, nothing like that comes.

So personally, after creating hundreds of affiliate websites, I will recommend you to stay away from the free hosting and rather invest a few dollars in a paid hosting plan.

Since you are investing time and energy in this affiliate website, and the ultimate goal is to make money from your website, you need to invest a few dollars for a paid hosting plan.

After my 7+ years of experience in affiliate marketing, the one recommendation that I can give you is to invest a few dollars in a paid hosting plan, so that you can beat your competition and drive much more traffic so that you can make much more money for your website.

With the paid hosting plan you will be getting unlimited space and unlimited bandwidth.

You can drive as many people to your website as you want.

Yes, some hosting gives you an upper limit of 10 – 20,000 visitors per day.

But if you are just starting out, that is more than enough for you.

Also instead of worrying about installing WordPress or other technical difficulties, which we will be talking about later in the video, there's a one-click installation for everything.

All you have to do is click on a couple of icons and everything will be installed, automatically.

And the most important reason for going for a paid hosting plan is the support staff.

I can't tell you how important this is.

Even today after opening 50+ websites for myself and for my clients, still we face issues.

And the one thing that I have to do is, go to the support staff.

I tell them my issue and within a few minutes, everything is fixed.

There have been multiple instances when my websites were hacked.

And it was the support staff who helped me out.

And also paid hosting plans used to be expensive earlier.

Now, they're extremely cheap.

And if you're following our affiliate marketing mastery course and if you are creating an affiliate website like the way I tell you, then within few months, you will be making money from your site.

So the money that you are investing in your hosting is not an expense.

Rather an investment, that will give benefits later.

So the hosting company that I recommend is SiteGround.

This is the company that I am using and all my affiliate websites are hosted in the same hosting company.

And I have tried almost all hosting companies out there.

Be it GoDaddy, be it BlueHost or HostGator.

I have tried them all.

But my search ended at SiteGround, this hosting company is phenomenal.

I even wrote a comprehensive article why I recommend Site-Ground, you can click on the "I" button here and check the article.

Also, if you'll be using our affiliate link to purchase the Site-Ground hosting, and send us the hosting receipt, we will be giving you a paid theme which is worth $50.

I myself use this theme for all my affiliate websites, because this theme is ultra lightweight, and your website will be loading at a lightning speed.

And Google use preference to fast loading websites.

So ranking number one on Google will be much more easier for you.

So now let's go into my laptop screen where I'll be showing you everything on how to purchase the hosting, how to configure your theme, how to claim these paid plugins and theme for free and how to configure your website like a pro.

Hey guys, as I mentioned earlier that if you're using my affiliate link to purchase the hosting then we are giving away 2 amazing things to you for FREE.

So first is this GeneratePress theme, this theme is already free, but its premium feature is for $49.95.

This is the theme that I use for all my affiliate websites, the reason is that this theme is ultra lightweight and it's very simple to use, very user-friendly and also very Google search engine-friendly.

So your website will be ranking at a much higher rate compared to your competitors.

So we will be giving you this $50 theme for free if you are using my affiliate link to purchase the SiteGround hosting and sending us the hosting receipt.

And the second amazing thing that we are giving is WP Rocket plugin.

This plugin will make your website ultrafast and your website will be loading at lightning speed.

And the best part is this plugin is so easy to use, you don't need to have any technical knowledge on how to make a website fast.

All you have to do is just activate the plugin and your website will instantly be loading in a very, very fast speed.

Now one website license for this plugin is also for $49.

Now I recommend SiteGround hosting and I also mentioned multiple reasons why I recommend SiteGround hosting and why all my websites are hosted at SiteGround hosting, so you can check the article here, "My Top 10 Reasons".

Where I have given you a comprehensive reason why I have recommended SiteGround hosting.

And why this is the best hosting for any Amazon affiliate website.

Now in the niche research video of this playlist, I showed you how to look for the perfect low competition, high-profitable niche.

So I have decided to go into the DSLR niche, just for the test purpose of showing you how to create a website and how to optimize it in a perfect manner, so I'll be creating a DSLR related website.

So let's search for a good domain name for this.

I'm searching for domain name, "bestdslrindia.in" Let's see if it's available or not.

Sometimes it takes a little longer to search for it so just, wait for it for a few seconds.

So the "bestdslr...in" is not available, it's already taken.

So let's try some other variation.

The reason why I'm going with the ".in" domain extension is because I want to target the Indian market.

If you go for the ".com" then you will be targeting the global audience and also the US market.

So, if you're targeting the Indian market go for the ".in" domain extension, if you're targeting the US market then go for the ".com" extension.

You can also go to the "My Tool" section, where I recommend all the tools that I use to run my online businesses.

And the first thing is definitely SiteGroundyou can also click here to visit the SiteGround hosting, so once you visit SiteGround hosting all you have to do is... so there are 3 plans.

There's a StartUp plan, the GrowBig plan and there's a GoGeek plan.

The primary difference between the 3 is that with the StartUp plan, is the cheapest but only 1 website can be built on a single hosting.

So let's say after a couple of months you want to create 2 or 3 more websites.

Then for every new website you have to buy a new hosting.

So that's the drawback of StartUp plan.

But if you go with the GrowBig plan, then you can create unlimited websites on a single hosting.

Like it says, it's unlimited websites.

Also the bandwidth of this hosting is really high.

So the website can easily handle 25,000 visitors per month.

But since I'll be giving you this amazing WP Rocket plugin and also this amazing lightweight theme, and if you're installing both these themes on your hosting, then you can easily handle 100,000 visitors per month.

Because I've been using SiteGround for many years now, I know... and I have used GrowBig plan as well.

And my website was easily able to handle 100,000 visitors per month.

So the one I recommend is GrowBig.

You can go for GoGeek, but it will be too expensive for you.

And also if you're just a beginner then GoGeek is not suited for you, rather go with the GrowBig plan.

So click here and get plan.

So now you have to find a new domain name, if you've seen my niche video of the affiliate marketing playlist where I showed you how to find a low competition high profitable niche for your website, then I showed you various ways to find a good niche for your Amazon affiliate website.

I have decided to go into the DSLR niche, because the profitability is really high.

Yes, the competition is also high, but I have a team of people who will be doing SEO for the website.

I have decided to go into the DSLR niche for the website, just for the test purpose, because I won't be scaling this website rather this is just to show you how to create an Amazon affiliate website.

So let's search for a good domain name.

"bestdslr..."

I'll go with the ".in" domain extension.

Because- since if you're targeting the Indian audience then go for the ".in" extension it will help you in SEO.

If you are targeting the US or the global market then go for the ".com".

But don't go for ".in" or ".org" etc.

Either go for the country specific domain extension or go for the global ".com".

So let's see that- whether it's available or not.

One recommendation that I can give you is in your domain name, make sure you have your category or the niche of your website or the keyword.

So my category or the niche of my website is DSLR, so I've added the word "DSLR" on the domain name.

Because this will really help in the SEO or the search engine optimization of your website later.

So if your website is about guitars, make sure you have "guitar" in the domain name.

Like "bestguitar.in" or something like that.

So now, I'll fill in all these information and buy this hosting plan.

One thing that you have to keep in mind that you- there's an option in SiteGround the "SG Site Scanner", you don't need it.

And apart from that, for the data center, take the data center that is closer to your target audience.

So our audience will be in India, and Singapore is the closest data center.

This is where all your files are hosted.

But if you're targeting the US audience then go for the Chicago data center because it will be closer to your US audience.

Similarly if you are going for Europe or anything else, then you can select the appropriate data center.

Since we'll be targeting India, I'll be going for Singapore.

So what I'll do is I'll fill-in all these information and purchase this hosting, So I purchased the domain name, "technewser.in" So now let's configure the domain name, configure the website, install WordPress and set it up like a pro.

So in the email that you used to purchase this hosting, you must have received an email from SiteGround, so open that email.

So as you can see I have received an email from SiteGround here, "sales receipt" so you open it.

And to claim the paid theme and plugin for free, all you have to do is forward this email to my email ID, which is "contact@ankuraggarwal.in" And just write down, "affiliate hosting receipt"... or rather also add the word "Amazon".

Affiliate hosting receipt- and send it to me.

Once we see this hosting receipt and we see that the sales has been generated from our affiliate link, I will give you the paid theme and the paid plugin and I'll also show you how to install both of these on your theme.

Go to your SiteGround account, open it.

And now, there are three options.

"Start a new website" "transfer a website" "don't need help now".

So start a new website, we don't have to.

Transfer a website if you're using- if you already have a website on a different host like GoDaddy Host, HostGater or BlueHost.

I highly recommend you guys to transfer to SiteGround because this will drastically improve the free traffic of your website, that is the SEO of your website, and will drive much more traffic.

I don't need any help right now because I will be showing you everything, how to setup manually.

And you don't need this SG site scanner it's not worth it, so confirm, and I confirm… and complete setup.

So this is the backend of your SiteGround hosting so this is how it looks, there's many options here you can increase more- you can upgrade the hosting, here's the billing, here you can access the support tab if you have any queries and few perks as well.

So the first thing is you have to go to "My Account" section.

So here's the entire detail about your hosting account and domain name.

So I have my domain name "bestdslr.in" here, and these are the other details regarding my hosting.

Like my IP address, my DNS, etc.

So all you have to do is click here "Go to cPanel", and "yes, proceed".

Now these are the details of your entire hosting account.

Like the domains you have added, the files you can access the files here.

You can access any customization that you need to do on your website on your hosting, you have to do it from this cPanel account.

So the first step is- as you can see that you have purchased the GrowBig plan on SiteGround and this is the main server of your SiteGround and the date and other information.

Now as you can see that SiteGround hosting has this lock here.

It means that the website is hosted on a "https" server.

Now you must have seen that Google has come up with various other announcements that they are preferring https websites compared to http.

So if you want more SEO traffic, more organic traffic to your website you need to install a "https".

Now other hosting provider sell it for another monthly charge, but in SiteGround, it comes for free.

So all you have to do is "Ctrl + F" (find), search for "let"... let's find where's Let's Encrypt.

Okay, here it is.

So... click here on Let's Encrypt.

Here you can see the domain name, "Let's Encrypt SSL" So you have to install it.

So select the domain name, it is already selected, then click on "install".

It is added in the installation cue and within few minutes it will be installed automatically.

So let's go back to the cPanel and now it's time to install the WordPress on your domain name.

So way to install WordPress is, click here on WordPress.

Click on install... you don't have to- keep it on 5.1.1 itself and the protocol you would want "https://www."

Because you just installed the https protocol on your website.

This is the domain name, directory you'll keep it empty.

For the site name I'll just add the domain name as of now "Best DSLR".

For the site description, we can add something like, "Best camera reviews on the internet".

Enable multisite, no... admin- this is the admin username and password, you can keep it anything.

So I'll keep it like "test" here.

And for the password, I'll keep it "test 123" Obviously you should have a different username.

And make the password extremely strong because WordPress is prone to getting hacked.

So make sure your password is really strong as well.

I have just used it for test purpose.

And for the admin email, add your main email.

Which will be used... so any communication or any contact form submission from your website will be redirected to this particular address.

So I'll be adding my email address- same that I used to purchase this hosting.

Select language, English... limit login attempts (loginizer), yes you would want this plugin.

And part from that, these are the options that you have to do.

And click on, install.

Oh, the password must be- see they reminded me.

So let's add... test_0709 maybe.

Okay, it's good under 50, it's good with 50 now.

So test_0709, let's install it now.

So now the WordPress is getting installed.

So guys, WordPress is installed now, let's open the website and see if everything is fine or not.

Yes, the website is opening correctly.

And also you can see that we have this lock that means that the https is perfectly installed.

So that's one good benefit of buying the SiteGround hosting that you get it- that you can get the https certificate for free.

And to install the backend of your website that is the WordPress backend, the WordPress dashboard, all you have to do is add this word "wp-admin" in the domain name of your website.

So I'll just click here and this is the backend.

So, this is the backend of your website, this is where you will be customizing your entire theme, adding plugins, changing the structure of your website, changing the look of your website, installing the recommended plugins, themes etc. and everything else.

We will be going through all of that in the latter part of this video.

Now here you clicked on this particular URL and you were automatically logged into your WordPress dashboard, but usually the username and the password that we created to install the WordPress, you have to enter it.

In order to access this particular dashboard.

So I'll just give you an overview of the dashboard, how it works if you're new to this.

So click here, "don't show this again".

Also there are few things that you need to do, okay, so I'll just give you a general overview.

This is the homepage of your dashboard, so this will- you can customize it if you want as well.

So this is the post section, this is where you will be adding the articles for your website.

So "All Posts" are all the published posts and the draft posts as well.

"Add New" is whenever you'll be adding a new article.

So you can click here, and you can add a title, you can add a description and everything else for your article.

Like this will be title, this is the description and the text size, color setting, advance categories, etc.

Similarly, you have the categories.

You can also segment the categories, like if- you have- my website is about DSLR, then I can create multiple categories like camera, lenses, camera accessories, etc.

And whenever I am writing an article I can assign a particular category to that article.

So that the segmentation is proper on the website.

Similarly you can add particular tags as well.

Whatever videos you're uploading, whatever images you are uploading it will be in the media section here.

In the pages section you will be creating pages like "About Us" or "Contact Me" etc… the "Terms & Conditions" the disclaimer, etc.

These are the pages that we will be creating.

Comment section is where all the comment sections will show.

If anyone comments, you can moderate them as well.

You can approve them, you can delete them, so all the comments will be showed here.

Plugins section, we will be going through that in a few seconds.

I'm just showing you all the recommended plugins that you have to install.

Users is all the users that you want to create if you want to give access of your WordPress dashboard to multiple people.

You can create moderators, you can create editors, you can create administrators, so all of that...

Similarly tools is for- if you already have some files you want to import or if you want to export the configuration of your dashboard you can export it as well.

You won't be using this particular option very often.

Setting part will definitely will be- let's start on the setting part here.

So there are few things that you need to do on the setting part.

First of all add a proper tagline, your tagline should have your primary keyword.

So let's say your website is about DSLR camera review then you must enter "best camera review on the internet".

My main keyword "best camera review" or "best dslr" is already on the site tagline, this helps in the SEO part.

This is automatically filled, you don't have to worry much about it.

So I'll just save it.

Then go into the writing section.

Default post category and categorized- just keep it the way it is.

You don't have to change anything in that.

Just change it to "Summary" here and never check this option, it should always be unchecked otherwise your website won't be getting index.

So just change from full text to summary.

Click save changes.

Go to the discussion tab, you don't have to change anything here.

In the permalinks section you have to make sure that the post name is selected.

This is extremely important for correct SEO of your website.

So make sure you change it to post name and save changes.

So now that you have saved your settings... now let's install the theme that I was recommending you earlier.

So now that you have saved your setting now let's install a beautiful theme on your website which is lightweight.

And as I was saying earlier if you are using my affiliate link to purchase your SiteGround hosting and sending us the hosting receipt, we will be giving you this paid theme for free, this GeneratePress for free.

So all you have to do is, after you send us the hosting receipt, on the same email I will reply you the files of this theme.

So what you have to do is go to themes.

Appearance, themes section.

Click on "add new", "upload theme", "choose file" and scroll "generate press", select, open and install now.

I will be giving you the RAR file in the reply of the email on the hosting receipt that you sent me.

Once this theme is installed, click "activate".

Now the theme is active, let's see how it looks.

Yes, the website theme is active now.

And also, to get the premium features of this theme you also need to install one more thing.

So click on plugins, click on add new, upload plugin, choose file, I will be sending you this particular RAR file "gp-premium" click on open and click on install now.

And click on activate plugin.

Also activate the copyright- and this depends on you what kind of functionality you want from your theme.

The more modules you activate, the slower your website will get.

So try to keep your modules as low as possible and only keep the necessary ones.

So to check the overall features of the module all you have to do is go to "generatepress.com" and see the video overview of each module and see if you want it or not.

So now let's install the WP Rocket that I was telling you about.

How to make your website extremely fast, so if you are using my affiliate link to purchase the hosting and sending us the hosting receipt.

So we will be giving you the RAR file and the license key for this particular theme.

Along with that I will also be giving you the license key and the RAR file for the WP Rocket plugin.

So to install this plugin go to plugins > add new > upload plugin > choose file... I will be sending you this RAR file, select it > open > install now > activate plugin.

Now the thing is whenever you are buying a SiteGround hosting, it automatically installs a particular plugin called SG Optimizer, this helps in making your website faster.

But I have seen in my experience that whenever you are installing WP Rocket, WP Rocket makes your website much faster than the SG Optimizer.

And there's a clash of interest, so usually I deactivate the SG Optimizer plugin and only keep the WP Rocket.

Click on the- click on "clear cache".

Go to WP Rocket, click on settings, so now let me tell you the perfect settings for this WP Rocket plugin.

Go to cache section, enable caching for mobile devices, keep it this way.

File optimization, select "Minify HTML" "Remove query strings…"

"Minify CSS" activate minify c- "Combine CSS…"

So activate everything.

"Minify JavaScript" "Load JavaScript deferred" "Combine Java-Script" Now these are all the options that will make your web-site, extremely fast.

Save it, let's see if the website looks fine or not, or if there's an issue- it looks fine.

So no issue on that.

Let's go to media, click enable for images, enable for iframes and videos, replace YouTube iframe with preview images, disable-save changes.

Preload, it's fine.

Advanced rules- no we don't need it.

Database, looks fine.

CDN etc…

image optimization, no you don't need it.

So this is the primary configuration of WP Rocket.

So that's the best part of using WP Rocket.

You just have to press a few buttons and everything is configured automatically.

Whenever you want to increase the website speed- the website loading speed of your blog, it becomes extremely difficult be-cause you need to know so many advanced things like this minify, preload, CSS optimization and JavaScript optimization and it be-comes really confusing for beginners.

But whenever you are using a WP Rocket plugin, all you have to do is just like what we did a few minutes earlier, you just press a few buttons and everything is perfect.

Now our website must be loading at lightning speed.

So let's see the loading speed of our website on a good- let's see the loading speed of our website.

Ctrl + V (paste), I'll select a server which is closest to India that is Asia Japan.

So Pingdom is currently testing the website.

So let's see how long it takes.

So as you can see the website took only 1.14s load time and the performance grade was capital A 98, that's really, really good.

And the page size is only 24.2KB.

So here the website is loading in lightning speed but this is only because of WP Rocket plugin.

So that's the power of WP Rocket.

So now let's talk about making this website look nice.

All you have to do is go to the appearance section and go to the customize section.

This is where you will be able to access all the settings related to your website theme.

Changing the title, changing the widgets and all of that.

So let's go to the widget section.

Right side bar... so I don't want the recent comments section, I'll remove that.

Recent posts, maybe I'll keep it.

Archive I'll remove.

Categories, I'll remove.

Meta, I'll remove.

Search, I'll keep that.

So make sure you publish everything otherwise it won't be saved.

Let's go to the footer widget.

Whether you want to keep the footer widget or not.

And the best part is you can click anywhere to access the edit of that particular area of the theme.

So I just click here and I can see that I am in the copyright area now.

Okay, similarly you can configure anything related to your blog.

Now I won't be gong through each and every option of the blog otherwise it will take at least an hour more, just to configure the website.

And I'll keep this part unto you, on how to do it.

So I want you guys to read the documentation of this particular theme, and go through each option and- like here you can select the logo of your website and the site icon and everything.

The layouts, the color, the typography... I won't be giving you one specific way to do it because then all the people watching this video course will make the same type of website, I don't want that.

So I recommend you guys to read the documentation.

It's pretty simple, it's not that difficult if you have created a website and- it won't be- and also there are a lot of YouTube videos regarding the GeneratePress theme.

So you can watch all of them and configure your website with the way and the look you want.

And also make sure you share your website look on the Facebook group.

Learn Digital Marketing with Ankur Aggarwal group, and I'll give you feedback on your website and in your articles and everything.

So make sure you are active in the group as well.

So apart from that, you'll also need to install a couple more plugins which will really help you in your website.

So go to plugins > add new > Yoast SEO.

Install this Yoast SEO plugin this is extremely important, and also activate the plugin.

And you also have to add one more plugin, that is contact form.

So click on- "contact form", and install this plugin as well.

And activate this plugin as well.

So go to SEO on the general section here.

You don't want text link counter, XML sitemaps... you don't want this "Rye Integration" because it's not worth it.

And apart from that, just click on save changes.

Search appearances, so make sure in the post section- settings for post URLs it looks something like this.

Go to the "Tax" section category in the search results- you don't want the category in the search results.

Because that is not good for SEO.

Make sure you disable it to "no".

And content URLs, remove the categories prefix... so just click on save changes.

Similarly archives, you don't want the author archives to be in the search results.

You don't want that, that's not good for your SEO.

Data archive, you don't want that.

Special pages...it's fine.

Click on save changes.

Similarly, media and the content type... let's see, post URL- that's fine.

Media it's fine, taxonomies don't want, archives... breadcrumbs... and general.

So this is what you need to do for the search console.

And anything else you don't need much of that.

So this is the setting of the Yoast SEO.

And...

Now there are few mandatory webpages that you need on your website, whenever you are creating an Amazon affiliate website.

So now I'll just- Oh yeah, guys I have forgotten to mention one thing.

That when you go to the themes customization, like I mentioned- showed you earlier, go to the theme customization > widget section > footer bar and add a widget here.

And this widget will be text type.

And just write this in your widget.

So here it says that BestDslr.in is a participant in the Amazon Services LCC Associates Program, an affiliate advertising program designed to provide a means for sites to earn advertising fees by advertising fees etc.

So in this particular- just replace the "BestDslr.in" here and here, with your domain name, whatever you choose.

So this is a mandatory requirement for Amazon associate account, so whenever you are creating an account you need this on all pages of your website.

That is the reason we have added it to our footer bar.

So that it is visible in all the pages.

Otherwise your account will be banned.

So make sure you do this and click on publish.

So now let us go to the pages section here.

You also need a few mandatory pages on your website.

So we'll create a few pages.

So the first page is "About (Your Website Name)", or you can directly create an "about" page.

And write few sentences here like what your website is about.

Like for me the website is about premiere camera reviews, and how is our research process... like, what makes us different.

So a little story about yourself.

And you can also check other Amazon affiliate website on the internet and see what kind of permission they have about the "about" section.

Apart from that you also need a "terms of service" page.

You'll need a "privacy policy" page, and a disclaimer page, right?

And the line that we copied earlier in the customized section, also make sure that this particular line is also added here in the disclaimer section as well.

So all these pages like about section, terms of service this- terms of service, privacy policy and disclaimer, you can create it after looking at the various other- because almost all websites have it.

So just look at the various pages of various websites, and just get an idea and create these three pages but make sure that the line that you have added here is also here in the disclaimer section because this really helps from not getting your Amazon account banned from the Amazon Associate account.

And also make sure all the links of these pages are publicly shown on the footer bar of your theme.

Because these pages should be directly accessible because whenever your account is getting approved, the Amazon Associate center will be checking whether these pages are available or not.

So make sure these pages are also available in the footer menu.

So this is what you need to do to configure your website.

So these are the few pages that you need to create.

Now you need some menu items, so go to the menu section here.

And here you can create multiple menus.

So I can create the top menu here.

So you can create it to be the primary menu... so let's first create some categories.

So let's say you have a category name like DSLR.

So create new category, you might also have DSLR accessories.

I'm not sure whether the spelling is correct or not.

But I'll just keep it right now.

And then you'll have some Lenses, right.

So add this category.

So this way you'll have multiple categories to segment your content, with these categories, you can create multiple menu items.

So we have- I have created this Top Menu, and I'll add this to primary menu.

I will select the categories that I have created.

I'll add DSLR, accessories- and add to menu.

This way you can create a menu item.

You can also create a home menu item.

Like, I can create a home menu item, and add the URL here.

Okay... then add to menu.

And keep it to the top.

Once you save the menu, and now when you'll visit your website, you'll have these menu items.

Like Home, DSLR, DSLR Accessories and Lenses, etc.

You can create many more items and if you're using GeneratPress then you'll also have the option for submenu if you enable that particular element, right?

So guys for the customization of the theme, I have kept it for yourself, because I want you guys to know your themes from in and out.

And this is why I recommend you guys to read the documentation of GeneratePress.

Because you are creating an Amazon affiliate site you need to know everything about your theme.

So I really request you guys to go through the entire documentation, all the elements, how they work… what is the function of each element.

And share the look of your website that you have created in our Facebook group so that I can give you feedback as well.

So this is how you create the menu items.

Again I'll show you how to make changes to your website, all you have to do is go to themes in the customize section, here you can have all the options you can change about your theme.

And everything is live preview, you can click here and I highly recommend you guys to watch some GeneratePress YouTube tutorials.

There are some really good tutorials out there which will show you exactly how to customize your theme.

So guys, apart from this the only part left is how to write an article.

And we will be covering that in a different separate video, where I will be showing you how to write a perfect SEO-friendly Amazon associate affiliate article so that you generate the maximum revenue.

So we have a separate video on that.

Where I'll be showing you the entire process.

So guys, this was it about how to purchase the hosting, how to customize your dashboard, WordPress dashboard and how to claim your 2 paid offers that we are promoting right now.

The theme and WP Rocket.

Your website is already loading at lightning speed.

And the only task for you guys is to customize your theme and make it really amazing.

The best recommendation that I can give you is watch the tutorials and also check the websites of your competitor, get some ideas and replicate that.

 So what are your next steps?

I show you how to scale an

Amazon affiliate website from $0 - $1,000 per month.

HOW TO CREATE BACKLINKS

I f you are struggling to build backlinks or drive free traffic to your website, then make sure you watch this video until the end.

Because I will be sharing my 100% working strategies that I have learned in dong SEO.

Apart from the other important metrics that I already have covered in my SEO , The higher the amount of high quality relevant backlinks that you have for your website, the easier it will be for you to beat your competition and rank number 1 for your target keywords.

Driving massive free traffic to your website will be a piece of cake if you learn the art of building backlinks.

Before moving forward, this video is lesson 8 of our free affiliate marketing mastery course.

And this course I share how to scale an Amazon affiliate website from $0 - $1,000/month.

I show you step-by-step on how you can create high quality backlinks for your website and drive massive traffic.

So in this video, I'll be talking more about backlinks, how to find backlink opportunities, how to create the backlinks, the best method and the best strategies.

Before I tell you about creating backlinks, I have to mention one thing.

That specifically in India, I have had so many interns and all the people are talking about "comment backlinks" "forum backlinks" and "directory submissions".

Honestly guys, these are the worse backlinks that you can make.

These used to work in 2011 and 2012.

But especially in 2020, none of these works.

And rather than help your website, these will rather give you a Google penalty.

And your website will get zero traffic.

So guys, please, please, please stay away from comment backlinks, or forum backlinks and directory submissions.

And all these digital marketing institutes are still teaching these methods.

So guys since you're my students, I highly recommend you guys to please stay away from such kinds of backlinks.

They're not worth it.

Since this video is part of our affiliate marketing mastery course, so let's see how to find the backlink opportunity for the same.

So let's say you are targeting an article like "best dslr in India".

To find the link opportunities, what you have to do is first search for your target keyword, let's say you are searching for "best dslr in India".

Open the article that Is ranking number one, copy the URL, open ahrefs, go to site explorer, add the URL here and click on search.

Now this will give you all the referring domains that are pointing to this particular article.

Now I am using ahrefs, I know it's a paid tool and not every one of you can afford it.

I will be showing you the free alternative as well which is Ubersuggest.

So let me first tell you about ahrefs.

Now this is the best technique to find backlink opportunities.

Now since these websites are already linking to your target article, it's much easier to email them, or contact this website and ask for a link to your website as well.

And also you have to make sure that all the links that you are building are "do-follow".

You can then export this list as well.

Here the anchor text is best DSLR.

So it's a keyword-reach anchor text and also the domain authority of the website that is referring to this particular article is also very high, 64 domain rank.

So definitely the website, the quality of the article- so one- whenever you are looking at backlink opportunity, you have to look at 3 factors.

First is the domain rank or the domain authority (DR).

Here the domain rank of this particular website, which is referring the backlink, you can see it's 64.

It's very high, that means that the quality of the backlink will be really high.

Secondly you have to look at the relevancy.

Here you can see that the article is referring, that is giving the backlinks as "best digital camera in India".

So definitely the relevancy is also very high because the backlinks are targeting towards the DSLR –related article, right?

So both these metrics are really amazing.

The domain rank and the relevancy.

The third thing that you have to look at is the anchor text.

Here, the anchor text is "Best DSLR" so the keyword that is used to make the backlink is the anchor text.

Similarly you can check all the other referring domain as well.

Then what you can do is just open the website here, find the email address.

To find the email address, there are multiple domain extensions.

You can also use a Google extension called "email hunter".

So all you have to do is find the email address of this website, and send them an email that you are also looking for a- that you have also written a high quality article and it will really be nice if they can link back to your article or any other they that they'll be able to link to your article.

And now since this website is a very high authority website, it's highly unlikely that they will reply to your email.

So guys, one thing I have to tell you is that creating backlinks is not that easy.

Because people think that creating backlinks is a piece of cake, but then again it's difficult especially in 2019 when backlink is becoming more like a price commodity.

So don't think that you'll be able to create hundreds of backlinks in few days.

It takes a lot of time and patience.

Like I use a particular software for sending all the emails.

I use a software called "ninjaoutreach". Earlier I used to use "Buzz-Stream" as well.

Both of these are paid tools.

These are used to send email scripts to thousands of people at a time.

And if you're looking for a free alternative, you can use "GMass".

It's a free alternative software.

With these tools, you can create various campaigns, various templates.

You can create- so like for this campaign I added 250 blogs in here and I sent them almost 165 emails were sent.

So what it does it- all of you have to do is add all the website, like here I can see, I can open this particular campaign.

So to all these websites here, my email was sent.

And I was asking them for a link one way or another and few of them replied to me and then my team handles them.

They give the follow-up, sometimes people ask for money, sometimes people ask for guest sometimes they just give the link just because the article has a really high quality.

So this is the software I use, it's called "ninjaoutreach".

I will be creating a very comprehensive tutorial on how to do this.

Apart from that you can also check YouTube videos on how to use "ninjaoutreach".

But this is a paid tool, you have to invest some money for that.

Second alternative is Buzzstream, it is also a very nice tool.

I used to use it early.

This is just an alternative for "ninjaoutreach".

If you are looking for a free alternative you can use GMass.

So guys the best technique is to look at your competitor's backlinks and pitch them to get your backlinks.

So now the next question in your mind will what exactly to email to these guys.

So I will be creating a repository… so for that I have created a PDF file where I have added all the email scripts that I am using to send to my prospects.

So to get that PDF file all you have to do is like the video, and comment on this video "yes, I want it".

And I will share the PDF with you in the description section of this video.

So if you're not using ahrefs, if you're not investing in ahrefs and you still want to build the backlinks so there is good news for you.

So there is this tool called Ubersuggest by Neil Patel.

Just until last night, they were not offering the backlink opportunity.

While I'm recording this video, just today they have launched the backlinks feature as well.

So here I can see that I've added this website called "techradar.com" I can see that for every article, like I'm in the top pages section, that in every article, how many backlinks that this article have.

So it has 225 backlinks.

All I have to find the backlink opportunity is click here on "view all".

So these are all the websites that are referring to this particular article.

Similarly you can do this for any articles on this particular domain.

You can also export these backlink opportunities to excel sheet and download it for later reference.

And it also gives the domain score like the authority power of the backlink and the link type, whether it's a textual backlink or an image backlink etc.

And also the anchor text, like what exactly is the keyword which is used to build the backlinks.

So guys, whenever I am building backlinks for my affiliate website.

My process is to first make a list of my competing domains.

People who are already ranking in Google search engine.

Then my next step is to take each domain, add it to the site explorer in ahrefs and download all the referring domains that are referring to this particular website.

Then I sort them from no-follow to do-follow.

Like, I only click the do-follow backlinks and then I add all those domain names in NinjaOutreach here.

And then I start sending them my emails script of asking for a backlink.

Honestly guys, I cannot give you a one best recipe for building backlinks that will work.

Also guys, very important tip.

Stay away from websites like Fiverr... when you'll be searching for "backlinks" here, they'll be so many options like "I will boost your Google ranking with SEO backlinks" and so many other shitty services.

Guys, trust me, these will not help your website.

Instead of helping your website, they will give you a Google penalty.

So stay away from these services which are very cheap.

Trust me, that is my experience talking, stay away from such services.

Similarly, there's another website called "SEOClerks".

They also offer backlinks.

Guys, these cheap backlinks are not worth it.

The best kind of backlink is one that is highly relevant to your article.

Which is coming from a high domain website, and also has a good anchor text.

Also there is something called PBN which is something called "private blog network".

Once you start building the backlinks, sooner or later you'll hear about PBN.

You can also buy PBN links to get your website ranked.

But this comes under the gray hat area or rather purely black hat.

So what this does is- you might be able to rank your website for a-maybe a month, a couple of months, so maybe even for a year.

But then again, it depends on the luck.

If a new Google update comes up and your PBN is blacklisted, then your website ranking will go to 0.

And also there are chances that your website ranking will never improve with PBN links.

So I will highly recommend to stay away from PBNs, or Fiverr links or SEOClerks links.

They will not help your website, they will rather give you a Google penalty.

So my best strategy is to first, go to ahrefs, add you competitor's URL here in the site explorer.

My strategy is to make a list of your competitor, and add their domain names one by one in ahrefs or Ubersuggest, whichever one you are using.

Download all their referring domains, and start emailing them one-by-one.

If you're using a free or alternative, you can use GMass.

If you're using automated software like me, you can use NInjaOutreach or BuzzStream.

And for all the email scripts that I am using to build backlinks, all you have to do is like the video, and subscribe to the channel and comment with "yes, I want it" and I will share all the email scripts, in the description section.

Now for the next technique to build backlinks, you need to put in some efforts in the beginning.

But it will drive you free traffic, as well as few initial backlinks, whenever you're building your first Amazon affiliate website.

So the technique is about creating a very comprehensive article on the top experts on your niche.

Your website could be on any niche.

It could be guitar niche, it could be fashion niche, or it could be dog niche or anything.

So the idea is to create a very comprehensive article of all the blogs that exist in the dog niche, or whatever niche your website is in and feature them in your article.

So for that, what you'll have to do first create an excel sheet like this.

So here, the last name, first name, contact, the email address, the URL of the website you'll be featuring and the type of website it is it could be blog, it could be commerce, etc.

We'll be focusing primarily on blog and the domain authority.

Because this is a very important metric.

We need backlinks from high authority websites, so that the backlink power is high.

So let's say your website is in the guitar niche.

So all you have to do is search "top guitar blogs" and open all the articles that rank.

Then what you have to do is, go through each of the blog that is listed on this article and add them to your excel sheet.

So like here, the first is premiere guitar.

So add the premiere guitar domain URL, type of the website it is, and also check the domain authority using all the extensions on the website.

Then find an email address.

So let's say if dwe go to the website, so we'll just- so let's say we just go to the website and we'll copy the URL.

We'll add this to our list here.

Similarly, we'll try to find the contact address.

So to find the contact address, there's a very amazing extension which is free.

All you have to do is search for "email hunter chrome" and click on this first result.

And add this extension to your chrome.

Add this extension and this will really help you in finding the email address of the majority of the websites.

Apart from that, you can also search for "contact" and check the contact page.

Most of the time, the email address will be present in the contact page as well.

Or you can use other extensions as well.

So this way all you have to do is, populate this excel sheet will all the blogs.

So from 1... to 2... to 3... to 4.

And that's- similarly make a list of at least 100 to 200 blogs here.

So not just this article, you should check all the articles which should feature the various guitar blogs.

So this way you'll have a very comprehensive list of your targets that you can focus on.

If you don't want to do this work yourself, you can also outsource this on any freelancing website like "Freelancer.in" or "Upwork".

Now the next step is to create the article.

This again you can write it yourself or again outsource it on iWriter.

Like the one I mentioned on another video.

So all you have to do is, for every URL here, just open the URL and make a short description, take a screenshot of the home page and similarly a short description about the website.

You can do it yourself or you can outsource it.

And this way you can add a very comprehensive article on your website, your affiliate website.

So this way you'll have a very comprehensive article of top expert blogs on your niche.

Your niche can be anything.

So once your article is done and published, now comes the part of promoting it and also getting backlinks for it.

So for that all you have to do is, once your article is published.

So there are few email scripts that you have to use.

Like in the sheet we also added the contact address here, right?

So this is where we'll be using it for all the people who have been featured on your article.

You have to email this email script to all of them.

Like email subject "we love your awesome blog!" and here, "hi, name- name of the person".

You'll be substituting the name field for the name here.

"Love what you're doing on the site name".

Here you'll be mentioning the site name.

Just wanted to give you the heads up that you were featured in my new article, add the article title here.

And the- your article link here... And I really hope it will deliver some new visitors to your site.

So this way in a way, you are boosting the ego of the other person... that they have been featured on your blog.

So everyone loves appreciation, so they are likely to share your article on various social media platforms and they would give you a reply.

There will also be people who will not be replying to your email.

So you can also send a follow up and I highly recommend you guys to do a follow up, because I've seen at least 20 – 30% people replying to me when I send the follow-up.

So in the follow up, you just have to send the "I was thinking about you" in the subject line.

Hi (name), just checking to see if you have received the last email that I sent you.

And again, mention the link.

So this way you'll be able to reach most of the bloggers that have been featured.

And either they will be replying to you or thanking you or some of them will even be sharing your article.

Now comes the backlinking part.

So using this technique you were able to build relationship with these few expert bloggers on your niche.

Now, all you have to do is send this particular email script to them.

Hi (name).

Glad you liked it.

I'm a big fan of your blog.

By the way, I'm still new to this whole blogging world and I would love to contribute a guest post on your blog.

Give them 3 ideas, some really good titles which they are more likely to approve on their website.

And this way you can do a guest posting on their site.

And in the guest post you can include a backlink to your homepage, or to an article that you are targeting.

 So I know this particular process is a little lengthy one because you have to first complete this excel sheet then you have to get this article written.

And then you have to promote it, send the emails.

But then again I have seen the conversion rate is comparatively higher, compared to the other methods that we do for backlink building.

 So this will really help you in getting those initial backlinks when your website is new.

And... so I highly recommend this technique.

One other thing that you can do is that you can also send a badge.

Like you can create a free badge on Canva.com.

You can add text here like top expert 2019, whatever year it is going.

Top dog food expert if your niche is dog food.

And you can also send this badge along with the email that you have been featured in the blog.

So many people add this badge on their homepage or on their site.

This again will help you get few backlinks.

If anyone embeds this badge on their website.

 So this was the technique of building backlinks to top experts kind of articles.

 So you can use this technique as well, whenever you are starting a new affiliate website.

Now the next technique will be guest posting and I love guest posting because the conversion rate of getting backlinks is comparatively higher, because you are also providing a high-quality content to the other person.

 So it's a win-win situation for both of the people.

So to find a guest-posting opportunity, all you have to do is enter the niche.

Your niche here- you can- your niche could be anything.

It could be guitar with the double quotes and the guest post.

So all these websites are accepting the guest post.

All you have to do is make a copy of this particular tab here, and you'll get a copy here.

And again, instead of this, we'll rename it to guest post opportunities.

And again, we'll make a comprehensive sheet of all the opportunities that we could find.

So go from each article by article.

Again you can do this yourself or you can outsource it through freelancers.

All you have to do is go to the website.

Go to the contact or the guest post here.

And you'll see that they might even have an email address, like here is the email address "josh@guitaradventures.com".

Copy it at the contact data, add the name like "Josh" the URL of the website, domain authority, etc.

Make sure you do ask comprehensive research as possible.

Try to find as many opportunities as you can find.

I'll recommend you guys to outsource this work by creating a video tutorial and outsourcing it for freelancing websites.

So once you have this done, all you have to do is send them emails for a guest posting page.

And in the guest posting page, you'll be asking them that you want to send a high quality article on their website and that in return you just want a do-follow back link.

I've seen that I have been able to convert 2 – 3 persons of my emails in to actual backlinks.

So guest posts is something that I highly recommend to you guys.

I will recommend you guys to start with the top expert, then also do the technique that I did in the start of this video, of looking at the backlinks of your competitors, while side by side doing the guest posting.

If you want my email template on how I build my guest post links on my website, then you can like and subscribe to the channel and comment "yes, I want it".

And I'll share all the email scripts that I've shared on this video and also many more emails that will really help you in building backlinks for your website.

Now the next technique is guestographic.

In guest posting you are sending an article to your website.

In guestographic you are sending an infographic.

So what to do is, create an amazing infographic on your website.

Honestly there's this amazing article by Backlinko.com on how to get backlinks using guestographics techniques.

I highly recommend you guys to read this entire article.

It's an amazing resource and I use this technique myself.

I know it will require you to create an amazing infographic but then again, creating backlinks is not that easy.

You need to invest some time, or energy or money.

If you want to scale an Amazon affiliate website.

So I highly recommend you guys to read this article on Back-linko.com on how to get backlinks.

Using the guestographics technique.

The technique is all about creating a high quality infographic and then promoting it, just like you are reaching out for a guest post.

And many of the websites will start giving you backlinks and then they'll feature your guestographics on their website.

The best part about guestographic is for guest post technique, you have to write a new article for every website.

But with the guestographic one infographic once, and you can get as many backlinks as possible using a single infographic.

So that's the best part about guestographic.

You can even go one step ahead if you can create an animatic infographic.

Now I know that creating something like this won't be possible if you don't have the design background, so you can outsource it and create an amazing infographic- animated infographic like this.

So creating backlinks will be much more easier if you go one step ahead and create something like this and do the outreach process and send those email scripts.

And many of the people will be happy to lend to you.

Like this is another amazing inforgraphic.

So find ideas on how you can create an animated infographic for your niche.

And then use the outreach process to build backlinks to your site.

And one last thing that I highly recommend you guys to do is go to this website, Backlinko.com.

And read all their articles.

Like go to the blog section and read all his articles.

Similarly go into "ahrefs.com/blog".

And read all these articles as well.

They have some really, really amazing tricks on how to build high quality backlinks.

And this will really improve your SEO game.

Similarly there is this 3rd website called "robbierichards.com".

And I highly recommend you guys to again visit and read all the articles of this website.

So these 3 websites, if you are reading all the articles, these are more than enough for you to find all the tactics that actually work in building backlinks.

These are the pros of SEO- these guys know how to rank their articles to number one for very, very high competitive keywords.

And guys, there is no magic ways to backlinks.

I cannot give you a list of websites where you can directly go and sign up to get backlinks.

Backlink is a very slow process.

I have a team of almost 9 people working for me just for SEO itself.

And trust me there are days when we are not even able to build single backlink.

Even with the 9 member team.

So if you're going the white hat way, if you're going with high quality and low quantity.

Then, it's a slow area.

But then again the results will be amazing, because once your website gets ranked, you will be getting the free traffic, for all the years to come.

So now let's go through the Top 10 SEO tips that you have to keep in mind, while building backlinks.

Number 1, focus on quality not on quantity.

One quality backlink is 100 times powerful than 1,000 low quality backlinks.

Number 2, focus more on do-follow backlinks and less on no-follow backlinks.

This does not mean that you won't be building nay no-follow backlinks, because even having 100% do-follow backlinks will look shady in the eyes of Google.

Number 3, have patience.

SEO is not a sprint, rather a marathon.

You cannot expect to see results in just few days, rather, the results will start coming after few months.

Number 4, don't just focus on off-page SEO or creating backlinks.

You should also your energy on on-page SEO.

Like writing an SEO-friendly article, internal linking and doing SEO audit.

Point number 5, a relevant article for a low quality website is more powerful, than a non-relevant backlink from a high-authority website.

Point number 6, don't create all your backlinks using the same anchor text.

Rather, diversify your anchor texts, throughout your backlinks.

Point number 7, don't buy backlinks from any of these services like Fiverr.com or SEOClerks.com.

Instead of helping your website, this shady backlinks will rather give you a penalty from Google.

Point number 8, I have seen in many YouTube videos who call themselves SEO gurus, they ask their viewers to go to the comment section and make comment backlinks.

Trust me guys, they are not worth it.

You should never make comment backlinks.

First of all, they are no-follow and they will not help your website, at all.

Point number 9, if you really want to be good at link-building, you have to invest some money on a good SEO tool.

The tool that I recommend and personally use is ahrefs.

This tool alone is helping me create backlinks for all my affiliate websites combined.

Point number 10, you should also have 20% of your overall back-links, pointing towards your homepage.

It's all about looking natural and organic.

If you are building all your backlinks to just the articles and not the homepage of your website, this looks shady.

 So make sure 20% of your backlinks are pointing towards your homepage and the rest 80% are pointing towards the, articles.

 So what are your next steps?

how to scale an Amazon affiliate website from $0 - $1,000/month.

HOW TO FIND MOST PROFITABLE NICHES

So what is a niche?

A niche is the main essence of your blog.

So if you're a guitarist and you start a blog about guitar, then the niche of your website will be "guitar".

Similarly if you find a website that talks only about dogs, then "dogs" will be the niche of the website.

Selecting a niche is easy.

But more important than selecting a niche, is selecting a profitable niche.

See, starting a blog requires hard work.

You can't just start a blog, write a few articles and expect to drive millions of visitors to your blog.

You need a proper strategy in order to scale a blog from 0 – 10,000 visitors per day.

And this is why we have created our free affiliate marketing mastery course, where I teach you all of that in a step-by-step manner.

And also you're spending significant amount of your time on your blog, so wouldn't you want to make money off your blog?

Most new bloggers make this mistake of starting a website on what they like.

And many years later they see good results.

And especially in 2020, where the competition is increasing by the day, you need a proper strategy in selecting a niche of your blog.

So watch this video until the end, and I can guarantee you will be able to find a profitable, money-making niche, with low competition for your blog.

Also, if you don't want to waste your time doing the niche research yourself, then you can get my excel sheet where I've already done comprehensive research on Amazon, in 50+ categories.

I've also categorized them into the commission you get, the competition level on the scale of 0 to 10, and whether you should go into that category or not.

So if you want this excel sheet, all you have to do is Review & comment with "Yes, I want it" in the review section below.

Once we hit 50 comments on this

book I will make the link of this excel sheet public in the description section of the book.

Since this is part of our free affiliate marketing mastery course, and I want all of you to make money on autopilot, I will be talking specifically about Amazon, and how to find a low competition, high-profitable category that you can promote.

A lot of you get stuck in the step of niche research.

And this step is extremely vital for the sectors of your affiliate website.

What should my website be about?

Which niche should I target?

This is the most common questions that I get in my live streams.

Before I take you into my laptop screen where I'll show you exactly how to find a low-competition, high-profitable niche, there are a few things that you have to keep in mind before selecting a niche.

The first step is to choose a niche that people are actually looking for.

I will be showing you later in the video how to find data for this.

What you don't want is to create an affiliate website about a topic that people are not even searching for.

Even if your article gets number one on Google.

But only 100 people are searching for it in the entire month.

You won't be able to make any money.

The second point is, choose something that has low competition.

Later in the video I will be showing you how to find a low competition niche, but as a general rule, don't go for a high competition keyword.

Especially when you're a single man army or you're a beginner.

I have a team of 9 people and experience of 7+ years in affiliate marketing and SEO.

So I can take the risk of going in a high competition niche.

But for you, in can result to loss of time and money.

For you, you might think that very big or popular niche like mobile, through that you'll be able to drive thousands and millions of people to your website and will be able to make much more money.

But then again the competition in this niche will be extremely high.

And the chances of you ranking number one on Google, will be extremely difficult and also it will take a very long time.

I want you guys to start making money on just few months, not in years.

So go for a low competition niche.

Now the third point is, choose something that you yourself like.

You will be spending a lot of time on your website, like configuring it, writing the articles, creating social media profile and a lot of time in doing the SEO of your website.

So if you yourself do not like the niche, then sooner or later you will lose the interest, and then you will say that this method does not work.

I want you to achieve success and I want you to make money of your affiliate website.

So trust me, go for a niche that you yourself like.

So if you don't like cats, don't go into a cat niche.

Rather if you are interested in technology then go for it, because then the work won't feel like a burden.

Think about the hobbies and what you like and that's a good place to start.

So guys the first step in finding the perfect niche for your first Amazon affiliate website, is to search for this, that is "Amazon affiliate commission" on Google.

And when you press "enter", all you have to do is open this page.

So this page contains the commission structure for various categories that are available on Amazon and how you can promote it, and what will be the commission that you will be getting on each category.

So if you're an Amazon affiliate and you are promoting let's say Kindle devices or ebooks, then the commission rate is 10%.

So the commission rate usually leads from 0 % - 10% on Amazon.

So whenever you are selecting a niche, the ultimate goal is to select a category where the commission rate is higher.

And also the average selling price of the product is also high.

So let's say you are selling a product of let's say Rs20,000 and the commission rate is let's say 10%.

Then you'll be making Rs2,000 as profit for each sale that you'll be generating.

But then again finding such a category is difficult because already too much competition is there in the high profit categories.

So in this video I'll be telling you how to do the niche research, how to find a low competition, high profitability niche for your first Amazon affiliate website.

So I recommend you guys go through all these categories and their commission rate, and also bookmark this page on your browser, because you'll be revisiting this page multiple times.

Majority of the people think they'll start promoting mobiles because it's a very common category and a lot of people will be buying it.

But then again you'll see that the commission rate on mobile is only 2.5%.

And also you have to make sure of one thing, that all the popular mobiles that are launched in the market, like OnePlus6 or any other new mobile that is very popular in the market, usually they are excluded from the affiliate program.

So if you are promoting any of these models, then you will only be getting 1% of the affiliate commission.

And these products are excluded from the affiliate program.

So if you are promoting any of this, then you won't be getting any commission.

So whenever you are promoting a mobile or a very popular product that is high in the market, make sure that it is not in this excluded product category otherwise you won't be making any commission.

So usually, whenever I am creating an Amazon affiliate website, I am usually looking up a commission rate from 4% - 8% or 10% if it's available.

So like a 4% category like mobile accessories or an 8% like health and personal care are also very popular.

Because more and more people are getting health conscious, so it's a good category.

And you can also go for apparel and shoes because the commission rate is 9% because fashion is something that is not going anywhere.

So, the first step is to go through this commission structure, the next step is to select few of the categories and start doing research.

So let's start with... okay, I'll take the musical instrument category here.

And it has 8% commission rate.

So let's do some initial research on Amazon on how the products are, what's the average selling price, etc.

Usually whenever you are creating an Amazon affiliate website, your ultimate goal will be to write an article which will be something like "Best XYZ".

So let's say if you're doing the niche research for a musical instrument website, then we might be looking for "Best Guitar" or any other musical instrument, right?

You can also do the category research by clicking here on "shop by category" and this will open up.

And here are also the other categories that are available on Amazon, this is another good way to find the other various categories like so let's say if you're going into the electronic section, then you can know that these are the various categories that are popular in the Indian market.

So similarly this really helps in finding the niche, because each of these categories can be a website for itself.

Like I can create an entire website only about headphones.

I can create an entire website only about, let's say furniture.

So these are the various niche that you can create a website on.

So we'll go to the musical instrument category, let's see how it performs.

We are at the musical instrument category, let's see the various products that are available and what are popular.

So primarily, people are looking for drum accessories, guitars, and... okay, keyboards as well.

So let's open few of these links.

Here you will also find various article ideas, because you can also write an article about guitar accessories or pianos.

So the ultimate goal is to also look at the average selling price of the products in this category.

As I said earlier, the higher the product price, the more profit you'll make as commission.

So let's go into the guitar section.

I can see that majority of the guitars are selling for- in the range of Rs2,000 – Rs4,000... we can also see guitars from Rs8,000, Rs6,000... So let's say the average price of the guitar is somewhere close to, let's say Rs4,000, okay?

So, we know that in musical instrument the commission rate is 8%.

So I have create this excel sheet.

So, let's go for... guitar.

So I've created this simple excel sheet just to do my niche re-search, you can do it yourself as well.

So I've added the category, the amount of traffic the article is re-ceiving, the conversion rate, etc.

So let me explain it to you.

So this is the category of whatever we are targeting, let's say we are targeting the guitar, and the other musical instruments.

Now, how to find the traffic for the number one article.

So what we'll do is we'll search for the keyword "best guitars on India" on Google search engine.

And we'll take the top result, let's take this top result.

Once you copy the URL you have to open a free tool by Niel Patel, it's called "ubbersuggest".

Search for it… open the free tool, it's free to use, and then the URL here… make sure the country selected is "English/India", and click on "search".

Then what you have to do is go to the "top pages" section, and search for the URL that you just copied.

So here- as I can see that the number one URL that is ranking is "13 Best Guitar Branch in India", the one that we copied… and approximately 779- this is the number, this is the traffic that we will be driving if we are ranking number one on Google search result for a target keyword.

You can also see the various other keywords for which your article will be ranking, which is just like the main keyword, like "best brand of guitar… best guitar brands, best guitar in India" this is ranking for number one- number four position.

So the actual traffic if you'll be ranking number one will be close to 1,000.

So what we'll do is we'll add this approximate traffic here… let's say 1,000 people visit your article every month.

And the conversion rate is usually 1%.

So let's say 1,000 people visit your article, then in my experience in running many affiliate websites, I've seen that 1% of the people tend to buy the product, the conversion rate will be 0.01, which is the one percent.

The average selling price of the guitar we saw that it is close to 4,000, and the commission rate was 8%.

So, my earnings from that particular article will be Rs3,200.

So I'll be making a commission of Rs3,200.

And you can see that the number of backlinks that this particular article has is 0.

So that even without backlinks, this article is ranking number one.

So the competition in this niche is "very low".

So ranking this article as number one on Google will be extremely easy.

Similarly I did a research on the DSLR category earlier, and I saw that the traffic potential for this article was close to 20,000, conversion rate 1%, average selling price of a DSLR is close to Rs30,000, the commission rate is 4%, so my earnings will be around R2s40,000 per month, if my article like "best DSLR in India" is ranking number one.

But then again the competition is very high, rather it's "very high".

Because the earning potential is very high, that is Rs240,000, that's why the competition is also very high.

So ranking this article as number one on Google will be difficult.

You won't be writing a single article on guitar.

So let's say if you're writing a guitar article for guitar like "best guitar in India".

Then your website will be in the music category or maybe the guitar category.

Then you can also write articles like "best electric guitars... best acoustic guitars..." You can also write articles about accessories, like "best guitar accessories..." And you can also write particular reviews about a very popular guitar.

So this is how you scale a website.

Your main article will be the best main category of your website, and then you can scale the website by adding more articles as related to the category.

Like if your website is more into the music instrument, then you can also go into the tabla, piano, or various other musical instruments as well.

Similarly if my website is in the DSLR category, I can also write many other articles like "best lenses, best camera accessories, best camera bags..." and so many other things.

So to find the article ideas for this, you can just go to Amazon and see.

Like I've just opened a musical instrument category here.

I can see so many article ideas like, best piano here, this might be something related to guitar, like best type of query for this... I can also write individual reviews, and add affiliate links in that as well.

I can also write articles about audio interface, DJ controllers and so many various things.

So this is how you do the niche research.

Let's do the niche research for one more category.

Let's go into the "books" category.

Okay, the commission rate is 8%.

So... let's go to... books, search for it.

The one good thing about books category is that the search volume is really high.

Because so many people are looking for a particular book review, or best books to read in 2019 or so many different queries for that.

And also the books category has various different subcategories like action, arts, and law...

literature, reference, religion- so many different categories.

You can create entire website just about book reviews, and add you book reviews in there.

But one thing that you have to keep in mind is that the price for books is very low.

So whenever you're doing your niche research with your excel sheet, the average selling price of a book will be something close to Rs300 – Rs200.

And even if the commission rate is 0.08, which is 8%, still you have to drive a lot of traffic that is at least close to 100,000, let's say the traffic is 100,000 and the conversion rate is 0.02.

Let's take a good conversion rate.

The money you'll be making, will be Rs32,000 per month.

So we are talking about books category here.

So let me give you a gist of the entire process once again.

All you have to do is first open this page of Amazon affiliate commission.

Go through various categories and the commission rate.

And also I recommend you guys to create this simple excel sheet for yourself as well.

I'll also make sure that I make this excel sheet available for download.

So all you have to do is after looking at the commission rate, start doing the research for individual categories.

So go to Amazon.in, click here on "shop by category"- various other categories will be shown.

Start doing research on the categories that you like one-by-one that has a good commission rate.

Once you select the category, look for the various articles that are ranking for that category.

Take the URL of the article that is already ranking, go to "ubbersuggest", that is the free tool by Niel Patel.

Add the domain name here… click on search, go to the "top pages", find the article, and look at this particular metric.

This is the estimated visit you will be driving.

Add that in the niche research here in the traffic area, add the conversion rate which is somewhere in the range of 1% - 2%.

Add the average selling price, add the commission rate and this will give you the oral earnings.

And for the competition, what you have to look at is the number of backlinks that the article has, which is ranking number one on Google search results.

So what you'll have to do is, do this for at least 10 – 15 categories that you like and that you think has good earning potential, and then look at the profit here.

Like which category has low competition, and higher earnings.

So whichever category has a low competition and high earnings, you can get into that category as the niche of the website.

And guys if you have any questions regarding this niche research you can ask on the comment section below and I will make sure that I will reply to you within 6 – 12 hours.

Just for example, I'm taking the case study of a very popular category like "best mobiles in India" when you search for this the main website- the most popular website that come on number 1 and 2 position are the "91mobiles" and "digit.in"

So I've added 91mobiles.in here in ubbersuggest.

I've gone in the top pages section, you'll see here that the popular articles are like "Samsung mobile price list…

Xiaomi mobile price list…" this particular article is "best mobile phones under Rs10,000".

And look at the traffic that this website is driving, 155,000 visitors per month.

And if we are looking at the 1% conversion rate we know that you'll be selling 1,553 mobiles at least from your article.

So if your article gets ranked number one on this article- so if your article on best mobile phones under Rs10,000 gets ranked number one, you'll be selling this many mobiles.

But then again the competition for this article is really high because you need high-quality 20 backlinks, and you're competing with a very high authority website which is 91mobiles.

So getting this article ranked will be extremely difficult, but then again the money you'll be getting will be good.

So this is how you have to do the niche research, you have to look at various niche which you like then you have to complete this excel sheet and this excel sheet will give you a clear picture on which niche you should go into.

So what are your next steps?

free affiliate marketing mastery course, where I show you how to scale an Amazon affiliate website from $0 - $1,000 per month.

HOW TO WRITE SEO FRIENDLY ARTICLE

I have mastered the writing of SEO-friendly articles. Even without backlinks, my articles are driving tons of traffic.

Yes, I know that creating backlinks are extremely important for getting your article ranked number 1 for your target keywords.

But in 2020 creating high-quality backlinks is extremely difficult.

But as you can see in the image on the screen that many if my articles are ranking number one even with very few backlinks.

So make sure you watch this video until the end because I will be sharing the exact strategy on how I write a perfect SEO-friendly article.

And you can replicate the same process for yourself, so that you can drive free traffic, even without backlinks.

Also I've created a checklist in which I shared the exact steps that you need to take whenever you are writing an article.

It also includes a couple more amazing techniques that are not shared in this video.

To get this checklist, all you have to do is like this video, subscribe to our channel and comment with "yes, I want it".

Once we reach a thousand likes, subscribers and comments, I'll share the link of this checklist publicly in the description section of this video.

This video is lesson 5 of our affiliate marketing mastery course, where I share how to scale an Amazon affiliate website from $0 - $1,000/month.

So if you've study my niche research process and the keyword research process then you'll know that yes, you need to be very cautious about the niche that you need to choose and also how to find a low competition keyword.

Because SEO is 2 ways, it's on-page SEO and off-page SEO.

Yes, you can build a lot of backlinks, but still you need to have that power of on-page SEO, so that even without backlinks you can get your article ranked number 1.

In my keyword research video, I showed you the example of best washing machines in India.

So let me search for this, and if we add the URL of the number 1 ranking page... let's say...

Bijili Bachao, this page is ranking number 1.

We add it here, go to search and go to top pages.

And click here, on "view all" for the article that we targeting like "best washing machines in India", this gives us the list of all the keywords for which this article is ranking.

Now we have to see that for this particular keyword, "best washing machine in India", this has the highest search volume of 14,800 and the position for this article, for this keyword is 2nd position, it is driving a massive 2,300 people to his website, right?

So our primary keyword becomes "best washing machine in India", right?

And our secondary keyword for which we have to optimize the same article is "washing machine best brands, best washing machine brand..." because the search volume for these keywords are lesser than this one.

And also the intent of our article is similar, because this is our direct competitor and Google is already loving it.

Then this guy must be doing something right.

So we'll keep our primary keyword as "best washing machine in India" If you are using Ubersuggest which is a free tool to find keywords, you can use that.

Otherwise you can use ahrefs, I've added the same article on ahrefs.

You can go to the organic keyword section.

Again we found the same keyword, "best washing machine in India" with the same 14,000 volume, approximately.

And similar traffic... so our primary keyword becomes "best washing machine in India", right?

So the first step of writing an SEO-friendly article is choosing the main keyword for which you want your article ranked.

In this case, we are choosing our main primary keyword as "best washing machine in India".

So let's go back to our WordPress dashboard, we'll add a new article.

And we'll add the title as the main keyword, which is "Best Washing Machine in India".

Now you have to understand, this title is only for our blog, right?

So the title that will be shown on the search result.

This title is shown which we add here in the meta description and the meta title.

This is the title here.

So if you add the "best washing machine in India" here, in the Yoast SEO plugin, this is the Yoast SEO plugin.

And whatever we write here, like... right now the month is April

2019 and let's say we write "Review and Comparison" because you are doing a complete review and comparison okay, we can also add a "Top 10".

We are doing a "Top 10 Best Washing Machine in India (April 2019) – Review and Comparison".

Now the title here might be "best washing machine in India", this is only for your blog.

But the title here, is the title which will be shown on the Google search results, right?

And you have to make sure it is green here.

If it goes red, that means the length of the title is higher than what is allowed.

So make sure the bar is green.

Okay... and the second step, is to have your main keyword, which is the "best washing machine in India" in the URL as well.

And the URL must contain only the main keyword.

That is this... "best washing machine in India".

And it should not have anything else.

This is the SEO tactic that I use, where I keep the URL with only the primary keyword.

Now I must tell you that we registered the domain name as "bestdslr.in" but this website I've created just for the dummy purpose, just to show you exactly how I write my articles, for my affiliate website.

I know it is not related, but this is just for the general purpose.

Okay guys, now comes the meta description.

So now we have added the meta title, we have our main keyword in the URL structure, now we must add a description which is enticing, and will give a reason for people to click.

Because this part of Yoast SEO is extremely important.

The title should be something for which the people would want to click.

Now we have added like, "Top 10 Best Washing Machine".

So someone who's searching for best washing machine like here we can see that majority of the results that are ranking are either top 5 or top 9 or top 10.

So we know this is the type of query and this is the kind of intent a person has when someone is searching for best washing machine in India.

So we'll try to follow.

Don't try to come up with something new, rather follow what is working and do better than your competition.

So majority of the people have Top 10 article, so we have done the top 10 thing.

We have added our main keyword, and we have also added the month and the year.

Because everyone wants to keep themselves updated with the latest information.

So by adding the word April 2019, will increase the rate of people clicking on our result compared to our competitor.

This will help in getting us better ranking.

And also adding review and comparison, we are again telling the person who is searching that we have done a detailed review and comparison.

Now we can add our very rich, meta description as well.

"We did comprehensive research on the best washing machines in India and came up with our final recommendations."

Or we can add something like, "If you are planning to buy a washing machine…" Okay so now the bar is orange, make sure it is only green.

So we have our main keyword "best washing machines in India" here, in our URL as well as our title.

Our title is very nice, it follows what is already working in the Google search results.

We have also added month and the year, so that our click-through rate increases.

And also we have added the "review & comparison" so that more and more people click on our title.

Okay?

So this is the part of the Yoast SEO.

Now, let's come- now let's check our competitors.

What kind of content they are writing.

So whatever your target keyword is, so make sure you search for it, and look at the articles of the top 5 people who are ranking for your target keyword.

So this is the research process.

Whenever you are thinking an SEO-friendly article, doesn't mean that you'll just think of an article and then write the article yourself.

You'll have to do proper research first, you have to look at your competition, what they are writing.

How they are writing the article, what is working, what is not working.

So that you can write an article, better than your competitor.

The ultimate goal of writing an SEO-friendly article is writing an article that is 10x better than all your competitions So we'll try to find troubles in each of the articles here, and try to write a better article than that.

So let's go to the first article here.

We can see that, he has a very long paragraph.

Now the thing is, no one wants to read a huge paragraph.

People prefer single-line answers.

Something like- something which has paragraphs.

Something which has indentation, like a one line or two line paragraph.

So one thing we can do is, we can add proper spacing.

Okay, so here is a little table of contents.

So that is good for navigation purpose.

So he has the keyword in the title, he has proper links, and he has shown the images.

And see again the paragraphs are too long, so it becomes boring.

So what we can do is, we can write the articles which has proper indentation and formatting.

Also I can see there's no pros and cons...okay, so here we have pros and cons... but then again, they are not properly segmented.

So we can improve on that.

And also I can see, there are no videos here.

So if you can find some YouTube videos, reviewing the images, that will really help in increasing the on-page time of our website.

And that will really help us get better rankings.

So let's go to the 2nd article.

Okay, so this article looks really nice because you can see there, the proper formatting, proper indentation, it also has table of contents.

And also proper- see the- he has the main keyword in the title of the article.

Like "best washing machine in India 2019".

Also he has really done- also he has really done good formatting.

Like he has blue boxes, with proper bullet points.

Proper indentation.

Also you can see that there's this "view on Amazon" on the image.

So this really help in increasing the total number of clicks towards Amazon.

Also the pros and cons look really nice... with the green checkmark and the red bar.

And... so this article is really nice, it looks really good.

But also this article doesn't have any videos.

So maybe that is the only improvement that we can do from this competition.

And one thing that you'll see that majority of the articles are really long.

So this means, that you will also have to write a very long article because people who are looking for best washing machines may be looking for very comprehensive information.

So, we'll also have to write a buyer's guide.

Like everyone else is doing, like... where we'll be explaining all the things related to washing machine.

Like, inverter technology, bubble wash... whatever it is- exactly it is.

And this person has also written a buyer's guide, like front load vs top load machines, etc.

So very nice written article, I really like this particular article.

Let's go to the next competitor.

Again, we have proper images, sources... and detail again top 10 type of article.

And information again on each one of them each of the machine.

And this article, doesn't have- it also has a buyer's guide.

So we now have a general idea of what kind of article is working on Google.

That for the top 10 best washing machine query, majority of the people are writing a top 10 article, with proper indentation, images, pros-cons and a buyer's guide.

So what you can do is- now you have 2 options.

Either you can write the article yourself, or you can outsource it.

Now if you are writing the article yourself, it will take a lot of time.

Because again we can see that majority of the competitors have written at least 4.000 or 5,000 words per article.

This is easily a 4,000-word article.

So you'll have to write at least 4 or 5,000 words.

And that too about a topic that is not too interesting.

So either you can write the article yourself, or you can outsource it.

If you're thinking of outsourcing it, then the company I recommend is definitely "iWriter".

Okay, so you're writing an article about "Top 10 Best Washing Machines In India", right?

So make sure- what would you like?

An article... it's more like informational article.

I guess... let's see... might be in home improvement.

I guess... we can select the category.

The category really doesn't matter.

Article enter keyword... you can write, "best washing machine in India" the keyword, for which the article will be optimized.

The word length, as you can see the competitors has almost 3,000 – 4,000 words.

So make sure you, at least select 4,000.

And writer level... the-

Now this is where the quality of the article comes.

If you go for the standard, the pricing will be much cheaper.

And if you go for the premium, it will be somewhere- somewhat fine.

So, if you go for elite, it will again be more expensive.

So I've seen that the premium articles are somewhat nicer, so you can go for a premium article, which will cost you around $66.

And here comes the project instructions.

Make sure you give detailed project instructions.

Don't be lazy on this, because the content writer which you'll be hiring, the more details you give him about the article, the better it is for him.

So I usually write my product instructions very carefully and very detailed.

So that the other person who's writing the article he has exact information about what kind of article, I have in my mind.

So also enable whatever option you think is will be relevant for the type of article like the objective, things to mention, sourcing requirements etc.

Like the tone of writing.

Okay... so let's say the company information..

it's not really required, so you don't need the company information.

But for the objective- like the sourcing requirements, you can mention here all the different URLs, like he must do comprehensive research on Amazon.in not Amazon.com because we are targeting only the Indian audience.

And also on YouTube to make the final list, right?

And you can also list all the URLs for reference.

Like the URLs of these, the competing domains.

You can add these URLs for reference as well, for the person to have a better idea.

Things to mention.

You can mention anything that is mandatory like you should also add YouTube links of all products.

Because that will really help us increase the on-page time of our website, by embedding the YouTube videos.

And things to mention, "also have proper formatting" and "write shorter paragraphs".

This will really help us increase the on-page time of our website, because no one wants to read a huge paragraph, everyone wants proper indentation, like the article I showed you here for this particular website Kitchenarena.in.

This article looks really nice, because it has proper formatting, proper images, indentation etc., right?

 Similarly you must also add the inform- objective like- inform and educate.

But our objective is "motivate and purchase" because we want people to- you know, go to the article and then they should buy the product from Amazon.com.

I'll also add an objective that "you are promoting affiliate links in this article, so make sure people are motivated enough to buy", right?

 So make sure you fill up all these boxes with the detailed information so that the content writer doesn't get confused.

Otherwise, the content quality won't be that good.

The more information you give, the better the content-quality will be.

There… so once you do all of these, you have to load the funds.

Once you add money to your account and then you can go to

place the order.

And within a couple of days, the content writer will give you the article.

And... then you have 2 options, it's not like the content writer delivers the article and you have to accept it.

You have 2 options, either you can accept the article if you like it, or you can give it for review as well.

Like if the content writer, maybe missed something.

Or you are not happy with the article, or you want something to be changed.

Then you can again give it back to the content writer, to edit it and give it back to you.

If you want to outsource your article, or if you want to write the article yourself, then we can do that as well.

So for writing the article yourself, I have already mentioned multiple things that... first of all there should be proper indentation, you should have images and also for all the images that you are adding to your article, make sure you compress them.

So for that, there's a website called "Compressjpeg" Go to the website, open the website... and whatever images you are uploading, let's say... okay, so let's download this particular image.

Keep it in the downloads folder.

And upload the image, and it is getting compressed.

So the image is compressed by 28%.

So the lighter your webpage is, the faster it will load and hence the better ranking you will get.

Because Google always wants a fast website.

Like if you've seen our how to set up the blog video, of this affiliate marketing playlist, when I gave you the WP Rocket plugin for free, right?

That plugin also increases the loading speed of your website, right?

Similarly, if you're compressing the images, there'll be less load on the server and hence your website will load faster.

So make sure you compress all the images that you are, uploading.

Apart from that whenever you are uploading an image, so let's say you download it, right?

And you add the image.

Upload... and this one is the downloaded one.

So make sure you also add the "Alt Text".

So this is a washing machine and we can also add a keyword here, like we can just copy the keyword from here and add the alt text.

This will also help in getting ranking in the Google image search, right?

You can also decrease the size like the medium size, as well as the indentation, as well.

Okay.

If you're writing an article about the "best type" query, then I highly recommend you guys that your article should look something like this, right?

It has proper indentation, table of contents, it has the main word in bold as well.

And also look at how he has added the main keyword for which he is targeting, in bold and in H2 heading.

So let's delete it.

So... le's say whatever you're writing.

"Today, I will help you find the best washing machine in India".

So one thing that you have to keep in mind, is that the main keyword should be in the intro.

That is should in the first 100 words of your article.

This will really help in the SEO of your website.

Okay.

Apart from that, your article must be 4,000 words or at least 3,000 words if you want to rank.

Because the competition is increasing day-by-day, so if you really want to rank, you need to write an article, which is very comprehensive, which contains all the information that the person is looking for.

And then you have to look at the intent of the person.

If the intent is getting fulfilled, he'll be happy, he'll be spending more time in your website and he won't be leaving it.

And then this gives the indication to Google, okay, this article is perfect.

This article is giving all the information that a person is looking for.

So this article must be good, so it will give you a better ranking on the Google search result.

Also guys, if you're using the GeneratePress theme, or if you're new to WordPress, I highly recommend you guys to play with all the options and- to be able to familiarize yourself with all the functionalities that WordPress has to offer.

Like you click here on + sign and see, there's so many options.

Like you can add a gallery, you can add a paragraph, image, list, quote, file... layout elements as well.

You can add a page break.

You can add a button.

You can add formatting, you can add comment blocks, and also add... like there's so many options.

So if you want your article to look something like this, you can easily create that in your WordPress, along with your Generate-Press theme.

You don't have to buy any expensive plugins or any expensive template, everything can be done through your WordPress or GeneratePress theme itself.

One more tip guys that I can give you about writing an SEO-friendly article is that you should not have any grammatical mistakes.

Because, whenever someone is searching for information, they come through an article which has a grammatical mistake, they end up not trusting the website.

And when the website is making grammatical mistakes, the person doesn't trust the website.

What will end up happening is, they'll hit the back button and they'll go to some other website.

So the best way to remove grammatical mistakes, is to go to "Grammarly".

Go to grammarly, it's a free writing assistant.

You don't have to pay anything to get your articles checked.

All you have to do is, once your article is done, copy the entire text, paste it here... it will give you all the recommendation about the grammatical mistakes you have, it will also show you the answer, how to improve it, how to correct it- So make sure you use Grammarly before publishing your article.

So this is another tip I have for you.

Apart from that guys, make sure you use proper heading structure.

Like this article, it has proper H2 headings, and H1 headings.

It has proper H3 headings... it has bullet points, it has pros-cons, beautiful colors.

And also if you look at the buyer's guide here, like here it is the H2 heading, again, there's an H3 heading.

Then H4 heading.

Again, H3 heading...

Similarly, make sure you sure you use a proper heading structure as well to get higher rankings.

And if you have any other questions regarding writing an SEO-friendly article, guys I- I highly recommend you guys to ask your questions in the comment section below, and I'll reply to you within 6 hours to 12 hours.

And I really want all of you guys to succeed with your Amazon affiliate sites and I really want you guys to reach the $1,000/month mark, form your first Amazon affiliate website.

So share your first article, whatever article you are writing, make sure you share it in the Facebook group, which is in the form of "Learn Digital Marketing with Ankur Aggarwal".

And I will review your article.

I will tell you what other mistakes and that, how you can improve it, and another very important thing guys, since we are doing Amazon affiliate, and we are writing article so that we can make money from Amazon affiliate, Amazon Associate Account wants that a website should have at least 5 – 10 articles, otherwise they won't approve your account.

So this is why I was telling you about the service, which is the iWriter.

Because- to join iWriter.

The link to this website is in the description section of this video.

And if you don't want to write the article yourself, you can give the contractor 5 – 10 articles here.

And within a couple of days, you'll have 5 – 10 articles.

Which you can then optimize and do SEO on, build the backlinks...

Watch our SEO videos of this playlist.

And build the backlinks and get it ranked.

Because, like for myself.

I don't have a very good writing skill.

So instead of doing it myself- so I have a 50+ content writing team.

Two whom I outsource my content requirements.

So that- because my expertise lie in SEO, and building backlinks and getting my websites ranked.

 So I know my strengths.

So that is why I outsource the work.

And focus entirely on building backlinks, doing the SEO of my website, and making money.

I have one more tip for you guys, which will really help in getting the article ranked number 1.

Is to do internal linking.

Once you follow the entire process that I just shared with you, on writing the perfect article... once the article is done, all you have to do is, internally link the article.

Let's say you want another link for this article.

So whichever article that you have that is related to washing machine on your website, all you have to do is... like after a couple of paragraphs, write a line like, "Make sure you also check our other amazing article on best washing machine in India", right?

And you can use this keyword, as the internal link to the article that you're targeting.

This will also help in getting a better ranking, because internal linking also passes on the link juice.

And it is not exactly powerful as backlink, but it will still really help you in getting your articles ranked.

So guys, this was it.

So I'll just give you a brief overview.

You have to write an article which is around 3 – 4,000 words.

The article structure should be something like this article from Kitchenarena, best washing machine... you can- even if you're writing an article about DSLR or any other category from Amazon, I highly recommend you guys to check this website for the article structure.

And your article should be something like this.

And you should have proper formatting, you should have proper heading, proper images, the images should be compressed, you should also add YouTube videos, and embed the videos for an increase on the on-page time.

And focus entirely on the user intent.

You should be able to fulfill the user intent.

Whenever someone is searching for best washing machine in India, they are looking to buy a washing machine.

So whenever they are going to an article, they want complete information.

Exactly what are the different kinds of washing machine, which is the best one that I recommend, if I am recommending something, why am I recommending something, what are the best features about the washing machine.

So once all your articles are done, all you have to do is add the links to Amazon.

Just like this guy is doing.

All you have to do is, add the links here it is the affiliate link.

All you have to do is "buy at Amazon..." After every product that you are recommending.

Add the link, buy at Amazon, or "check price at Amazon".

All these are affiliate links, whenever someone is clicking here they are going to Amazon for the affiliate link.

We will be talking about how to sign up on Amazon Associate, what are the approval process, how not to get banned on the next video.

So until then, I highly recommend you guys to at least get you 5 – 10 articles written.

So we will be talking about how to sign up on Amazon Associate, how to get approved, how to not get banned, so until then, I highly recommend you guys to publish at least 5 – 10 articles on your website.

So the process will be choosing a niche, doing keyword research, and writing and publishing the articles.

WHAT IS SEO

SEO, or search engine optimization.
What is it?
How should I learn it?
If you have a website or a blog but you're not driving traffic to it, or even if you have a YouTube channel but are struggling to get the views, then SEO will help you drive free traffic to your YouTube channel or your blog.
I am driving over 1M visitors or 100,000 people to my website every month.
And 90% of this traffic is free and it's coming from SEO.
So if you also want some kind of traffic for your blog or website, then make sure you watch this video until the end.
Because I will be sharing all the tips, tricks, and strategies that I have learned through 7 years of doing SEO for my websites.
This book is lesson 7 of our affiliate marketing mastery course, where I show you how to scale an Amazon affiliate website from $0 - $1,000/month.
I also created a step-by-step comprehensive checklist on how you can increase the traffic towards your blog form 0 to 5,000 visitors per day.
If you want this checklist, all you have to do is like the book, review, and comment with "yes, I want it".
Once we hit 50
comments in this book I'll link this checklist public in the description section of this video.
So now let's talk about SEO.
What is SEO?
So let's say you write a new article on your website.
To drive traffic or to promote your article there are 3 options.
The first option is that you can promote the link to this article on

a Facebook wall or in Facebook groups, or the link section of your Instagram bio.

Now since the majority of you don't have thousands of people who are following you, so the maximum number of people who might visit your article will be somewhere close to 100 or 200.

The second option is that you can run Facebook ads, Instagram ads, YouTube ads, and drive traffic towards your article.

But in this case, if you're not selling a product or a service, and driving traffic only towards your article, then you won't be able to do it profitably.

The last and most important traffic source is organic traffic.

The traffic that is coming from search engines.

Like Google, Yahoo, Bing, etc.

So the whole process of SEO is getting your articles or your website ranked number 1 for your target keywords on the Google search results.

I'm only talking about Google and not the other search engines like Yahoo or Bing.

This is because Google dominates the search engine market.

You only have to focus on Google.

Once you are ranked number 1 for your target keyword, you will start driving free traffic towards your website or your article.

It will be more beneficial for you if I don't talk more about theory but rather show you everything.

So let's go into my laptop screen, and if you watch this video until the end, I can guarantee you that you will know more about SEO than 99% of SEO experts out there in the market.

So whenever I am talking about SEO, I'm primarily talking only about Google because Google has 90% of the search engine space.

As you can see that Bing only has 2.45% of the search engine space and Yahoo!

At 1.82.

So primarily whenever we are talking about search engine optimization or SEO, we are targeting only Google because that is the dominant player in the market.

So for the people who are total beginners who don't know what SEO is, whenever you are searching for a keyword here like "best washing machine in India", so these are the listings, right?

So the process of SEO or search engine optimization is all about getting your article to the number 1, 2, or 3 positions.

The reason we want to get it to the top position is that majority of the click rate comes from the first 3 results.

So, has there been any time whenever you are searching for a particular keyword, it could be anything like "best movies in India" etc?

Have you ever gone to the second page?

I have the advanced settings where I am showing a hundred results per search page.

But the majority of the people have 10 results on the search result page.

So have you ever been to the second or third page?

And even if you have been then the percentage of the people who are visiting the second page is very, very low.

So the ultimate goal of the website is to get to the first result for their target keyword.

I'll show you this with one more example.

I have opened my ahrefs and using the same keyword "best washing machine in India".

If you'll go to the search results page here, so the first website that is ranking number 1, Biijilibachao.com, you can see that it's driving 15,000 SEO traffic for its target keyword.

And similarly, the first and the second-ranking is driving 12,000 and the website on the third-ranking is driving only 4,000.

So if you are a number 1 ranking and if you are a number 3 ranking, there is a huge shift in the amount of traffic you'll be driving to your website.

This is the reason why everyone is targeting the number 1 position.

Since the number 1 ranking is so important for any website, this is the reason why SEO is so competitive.

Now the website who is ranking number 1, gets the most traffic and hence the most profit.

And since this video is part of our affiliate marketing mastery course, your target should be to rank number 1 so that you can drive maximum traffic to your website, and hence make more money by selling more product on Amazon.

So now whenever we are talking about ranking number 1 200+ factors make up the entire process of getting your website ranked on number 1, for your target keywords.

Now if I'll be talking about all the 200 factors, then this video will easily extend to 3 – 4 hours, so I'll only be talking about the most important factors that make a significant impact on your ranking.

But before talking about that, let's talk about the types of SEO.

Primarily there are 4 types of SEO: white hat, black hat, grey hat, and negative SEO.

Now white hat SEO is what I recommend and what I use.

White hat SEO covers all the techniques that you can implement on your website.

So that your website gets on the number 1 position, and white hat SEO is what is recommended by Google to do.

To compare white hat SEO with black hat SEO, so black hat SEO contains all the negative techniques, that are shady and does not comply with the search engine guidelines.

And white-hat SEO is what complies with the search engine guidelines.

So let's say you write an article that is amazing, really comprehensive and it completes the user intent.

And let's say a particular magazine likes your article and it features your article and they mention your article in their article.

So this creates a backlink for your article.

Now, this is the white hat SEO, because this is done naturally.

You are not using a shady technique or kind of link buying, etc.

We'll be talking more about white hat SEO techniques later.

I have created a comprehensive video on how to create backlinks for your affiliate website, so you can watch it in our affiliate marketing mastery playlist.

In this video, I'll be talking about more of the on-page factor.

On how you can get your website ranked number 1 even without backlinks.

So make sure you watch this video until the end.

The grey hat SEO is in the middle of the white hat and black hat SEO.

I don't even recommend a grey hat as well.

And negative SEO is whenever one of your competitors builds wireframe or on links to your website.

So that your website gives you a penalty.

So this is what negative SEO is… We won't be talking more about- we won't be talking about negative SEO, rather I'll be giving you the best recommendation on how to get your website number one using just the on-page factors alone.

If you've seen my video on how to start an affiliate website on this affiliate marketing playlist, then you know that I've created a dummy website called "best DSLR.in" And if I check its speed form Asia server and start the test, you can see for yourself that my website is loading at only 1.77s.

So if your website is loading under 2s that is what is recommended.

And also I am using a very lightweight theme called Generate-Press.

If you want this paid theme and paid plugin for FREE, then watch my video on how to start an affiliate website, in my affiliate marketing mastery course.

So to make your website load faster will help you in getting your article number 1 ranked.

The next step is keyword research.

So whenever you are searching for anything on Google search engine like "best washing machine in India" in this case, so this becomes a keyword.

Now, whenever you are writing an article you need to do thorough keyword research.

Like I am using ahrefs here, as I showed you by adding the number 1 result for my target keyword here in the site explorer region.

And clicking here on the organic keywords.

I can find all the keywords for which this article is ranking.

And also the position associated with it.

For the best washing machine in India, it is ranking number 1.

"Best washing machine", ranking 3.

And also the search volume of the keyword.

Now since ahrefs is a paid tool you can also use Ubersuggest by Neil Patel.

It's a free tool and it also gives almost similar data.

So once you add the domain name, go to the "top pages" here you can see the article "best washing machine in India" click here on "view all".

And you'll be able to see all the keywords for which this article is ranking.

Now, ahrefs is a paid tool you do have to pay money for this, but Ubersuggest is a free tool.

So here you can also export the keyword list, by "export to CSV" and download it for yourself.

Now many of the YouTubers I've seen... they recommend so many different software and various other tools to find the keywords, but honestly, keyword research is not that complicated.

It's very simple.

All you have to do is... whatever article you are writing... maybe you're writing an article, let's say... best places in India.

Okay, so just search for it.

All you have to do is search for it.

Take the first article, whatever it is ranking on Google search engine, copy the URL, go to Ubersuggest or ahrefs, if you are using ahrefs go-to site explorer, paste, and enter.

If you're using Ubersuggest free tool, go to Ubersuggest add the domain name, make sure you select the country for which you are targeting, click on search.

With ahrefs, it's a one-step process because you'll- like here you can see the keywords for which the article is ranking.

I can get the keywords, I can also export it.

But for Ubersuggest you first have to go to "top pages" then you can find the article, whichever the article you are looking for and click here on the "view all" button and download the keywords.

I've also created a very comprehensive video on keyword research in this affiliate marketing mastery course.

I'll add the link to the description.

All the links that I'm mentioning here in the video, everything is in the description section, you guys.

So make sure you check the description section.

So whatever keyword you are targeting, make sure the difficulty is less.

So like, if you are using Ubersuggest you can see the SEO difficulty here, like 35, 43... so anything below 30 is good for a person who is single-handedly managing a website.

If you already have an SEO team managing your company, if you're working for a company, then you can even go for higher difficulty like 45 or 55, 65, etc.

If you are using ahrefs again, the keyword difficulty metric here is different from Ubersuggest.

So anything less than 20 is good for you.

So you don't have to worry much about it because you can single-handedly get that article ranked.

But anything above 20, you will need an SEO team.

If you are doing everything by yourself then you have to wait for a longer time because beating that competition will be much more difficult.

After selecting the keyword, the other important metric is how amazing your article is.

Like here I searched for the best washing machine in India.

So if you'll open the first link here... the first search result.

You'll see that this article is very comprehensive.

Just looking at the table of contents you'll see that they have recommended the top 5 models.

They have also written a very comprehensive buyer's guide.

So if I am searching for the best washing machine in India, then probably I am looking for a washing machine, right?

So I need more information.

So when I come into this article, I can see that I can see all the recommended washing machines.

Their features, their pros-cons-specs, etc.

With their images and also their link to Amazon if I want to buy them.

It also has a very comprehensive buying guide, "fully automatic vs semi-automatic" "front load vs top load".

So if I'm looking to buy a washing machine, all of my doubts are covered in this article.

So if I'm spending more time on this article, this reflects goodly in the eyes of Google.

Okay, someone who searched for this keyword, spent a lot of time on this article, then definitely must be liking the article and hence, I must promote this.

The other important thing about SEO is writing an amazing meta title.

Guys as you can see here, like if you're searching for "best washing machine in India" Let's say if you're ranking number 4 here, okay but you have an amazing meta title, that is click-worthy.

So let's say... this particular result, number 3.

It has 5 backlinks and you have 2 backlinks.

But if Google sees that the majority of the people clicks on the number 4 result, and end up spending a lot of time on your article, then Google will think, okay that this particular result might have fewer backlinks but people are liking it.

And hence it will promote your article into a better position even without the backlinks.

So now we can see there is a general trend in the logistical article.

That you have to write a top-10 type of article.

Here, this person has also added the year.

By adding the year, it has been seen that the CDR increases because people want the latest information.

What another thing that you can do is… If you've seen our book on the SEO article, I'll add the link to that in the description section of this book

I also mentioned that you can also write the month.

Like here if you can add like, let's say the month is April, right now.

So you can also say in April 2019.

This will give the idea to the person who's searching that okay, this article is the latest, and the chances of the person, click on your article will be higher.

Similarly, you can do the same things for your meta description as well.

Like creating click-worthy titles and creating a click-worthy meta description will help you get to the number 1 position.

So make sure your title is very enticing, make sure your title is very click-worthy.

Because if you can increase the CDR of your title, then you'll be able to rank on your target keywords even with fewer backlinks.

If you'll search for, let's say "coupon".

Usually, whenever you are searching for coupons you'll see that majority of the results have the month and the year.

And this is because all of these websites know that by adding the month and the year in the meta title, the CDR will increase.

This is the reason that you'll see that almost all the website, are using this technique.

Like here in "CouponDunia.in" you can also see "free delivery".

This will give one more reason for the person who's searching for this keyword to click on this link.

Okay, so the meta title is something that you have to keep changing and wearing every week and see which one is giving you the best results and which one is giving you the best CDR.

Like, look at this particular result, like if you're searching for a "Swiggy coupon".

Look at the result here, "Swiggy coupons & offers".

He has targeted the main keyword here, apart from that he has also written free delivery, and he has also mentioned, 50% off promo code.

Now, who doesn't want a 50% off promo code, right?

So creating a very enticing title will help you in increasing the CDR and hence getting your articles ranked.

But then again you have to make sure, if someone is clicking here and going to your article, they must also get whatever you are offering in the meta title.

Because otherwise, he'll just hit the back button, and he'll go to the next result.

And this instead of helping your website will rather give you a negative SEO.

Unless there's someone who clicks on the back button and clicks on the second result, instead of going to your website, he went to the second result.

So instead of helping your website, this will hurt your website more.

So make sure whatever you're offering in the meta title is also delivered in the article content.

So look at the various titles of the various other keywords.

Not just the "best washing machine".

You can also add various other categories, like best DSLR, best mobile phones.

And look at the theme of the meta titles have.

And then try to vary your meta title.

Apart from that, you should also do a very comprehensive SEO edit of your website.

So SEO audit is all about giving you the technical difficulty that your website has.

So maybe some of the images are not compressed, or maybe you have a broken link, so all the list of all the problems of your website, will be given to you by an SEO audit.

Ahrefs is what I use for my SEO audit, for all my affiliate websites. But if you are not willing to pay ahrefs, so this is another tool called "u".

It also has a free vs paid version.

You can use the free version also, to do the SEO audit.

I know SEO audit is a very complex and very advanced step when we talk about SEO.

But for all the people who are experienced in SEO and who are watching the video, they can do their SEO audit here.

So this will be all about the technical difficulty of your- maybe some internal link issues, some meta link issue,s or content length.

This will give you a comprehensive view of the SEO of your website.

Apart from that I also mentioned this in the various other videos of my channel.

That you should always compress the images that you're adding to your website.

So whatever images that you're adding to your website, make sure you first upload it to this website, "compressedjpeg.com" Upload the image and this will give you a compressed version, and then always upload the compressed version of your images to the website.

Because you would want your website to load at a lightning-fast speed.

So make sure your website is not heavy with content, heavy with the videos.

Since you are creating an affiliate website, there'll be a lot of images like this person has added all these images, right?

But in your article, you'll be adding a lot of images.

If you're writing a top 10 article then you'll be adding at least 10 articles of the product that you're recommending.

So make sure you compress all the images using the "compress jpeg" website.

So if you're following all the videos of our affiliate marketing mastery course then you know that various things matter on the overall SEO of your website.

First is the niche, that you have to go into a particular niche where the competition is low.

Second is the keyword research, you have to find the right keywords which have low competition and high profitability.

I have already discussed all of these in the various other videos of this playlist.

I'll be linking all the video links in the description section of this video, apart from that, the on-page SEO makes your website extremely fast.

Should you be writing SEO-friendly articles,

So what are your next steps?

Learn and apply all the complete affiliate marketing mastery course strategies that we are discussing in the book where I show you how to scale a website from $0 - $1,000/month.